Fragments of Her Healing

A Story of What We Carry and What We Learn

Fragments of Her Healing

A Story of What We Carry and What We Learn

Whitney Brown, Ph.D., LPC

Eighth Avenue Publishing, LLC
Louisiana

Copyright © 2026 by Whitney Brown, Ph.D., LPC

Published in the United States by
Eighth Avenue Publishing, LLC
Louisiana
www.eighthavenuepublishing.com

Cover design, Interior design, and Project editor: Whitney Brown, Ph.D., LPC

All rights reserved. No part of this book may be reproduced or transmitted in any form or by any means, electronic, mechanical, photocopying, recording, or by any information storage and retrieval system, except for brief quotations used in reviews or scholarly works, without prior written permission from the publisher.

This book contains personal narrative and educational material. It is not intended to replace therapy, diagnosis, or treatment by a licensed mental health professional. Readers experiencing distress are encouraged to seek professional support.

The author does not provide medical, psychological, or therapeutic advice through this publication, nor does the author recommend or prescribe any treatment, strategy, or action as a substitute for professional care. Any information presented is intended for general educational and personal insight only. If you choose to apply any material from this book to your life or emotional well-being, you agree that such choices are your responsibility, and the reader assumes full responsibility for any choices or outcomes resulting from the use of this material.

Library of Congress

Paperback ISBN: 979-8-9947238-0-7
E-book ISBN: 979-8-9947238-1-4

1st edition, April 2026

Printed in the United States of America

For the girl I used to be:

You carried more than anyone ever knew, yet you kept going. This book is for your courage, your softness, your survival, and every quiet step you took toward healing, even when you did not have the language for it.

For my daughter:

You are my reminder that healing creates room for new beginnings. Everything I chose to face, unlearn, and become, I chose so you would inherit a softer world than the one I knew. You are the proof that love can grow in places where pain once lived.

For every woman who has ever tried to rebuild herself from pieces:

May these pages remind you that you were never broken, only becoming.

Table of Contents

Prologue: A Look Back — 1

Chapter 1: The Last Straw — 7
   When Choosing Yourself is the Bravest Thing You Can Do — 12

Chapter 2: A Fatherless Daughter — 19
   Open Letter to My Father — 25
   No More Waiting at the Door — 27
   But What Does Moving on Really Look Like? — 32
   Therapist's Work for the Reader: For the Fatherless Daughter — 35

Chapter 3: Bruised Soul — 41
   This is Not Normal — 47

Chapter 4: The Blues — 51
   The Silence I Had to Unlearn — 57
   Therapist's Work for the Reader: Returning to the Root — 61

Chapter 5: Sixteen and Pregnant — 65
   This is Not the End of You — 69

Therapist's Work for the Reader:
Rewriting the Narrative   73

Chapter 6: Repeat Offender   **77**

Relationships 1 and 2   78

Relationship 3   80

Relationship 4   81

Relationship 5   82

Relationship 6   84

Until I Noticed the Pattern Was Me   89

Chapter 7: Blank Canvas   **93**

Therapist's Work for the Reader:
The New Me   99

Chapter 8: Closed for Business   **101**

When the Body Remembers What the Mind
Tries to Forget   106

Chapter 9: Revelations   **109**

Revelation 1: You Are Not Responsible for What Broke
You, But You Are Responsible for What You Build Next   111

Revelation 2: You Can't Heal in the Same Environment
That Made You Sick   113

Revelation 3: Healing Requires Telling the
Truth About Yourself   114

Revelation 4: Not Everything Deserves a Seat
at the Table of Your Life   116

Revelation 5: Being Chosen is Not the Same

as Being Valued	119
Revelation 6: She Kept Me Alive, But She Can't Take Me Any Further	121
Revelation 7: Peace Doesn't Just Happen, You Have to Cultivate It	124

Epilogue: What Came After	**127**
Appendix	**129**
Resources for Help	**130**
References	**131**
About the Author	**133**
Stay in Touch With Me	**135**
Also by the Author	**136**
Notes	**137**

Prologue

A Look Back

"Healing is not linear. It doesn't arrive neatly or all at once. It comes in fragments; some sharp, some tender, all necessary."

There comes a moment in every woman's life when she realizes she is tired. Not the kind of tired a nap can fix, but the kind that settles into her bones. It's a deep exhaustion of the heart, mind, and spirit. She grows weary of repeating the same cycles. Weary of tolerating what she never should have accepted. Weary of trying to convince others of her worth, while secretly questioning it herself. This moment doesn't always arrive with drama. Sometimes, it sneaks up quietly. A breakdown behind the steering wheel while the world outside keeps moving, or the silence after another betrayal when the room suddenly feels too heavy. Other times, it starts as a whisper, a soft warning that something has to change, until it grows louder, pressing against your chest, then bursts into a scream you can no longer ignore: *Enough is enough.*

That's where my journey began. Not with a neat new chapter or a master plan, but with the heavy realization that I couldn't keep living the way I was. For years, life felt like a loop: different faces, same disappointments; different scenarios, same emptiness. I became an expert at chasing milestones: the "right" job, the "right" man, the "right" opportunity. I convinced myself that if I checked enough boxes, wholeness would greet me on the other side. But it never did. Each accomplishment was like water cupped in my hands; it slipped through before I could even taste it. Every new chapter I thought would save me ended up being another distraction from a deeper truth: I was carrying wounds I had never named, let alone healed.

We all carry something, whether we admit it or not. I call it *the emotional backpack*: a silent, invisible weight we drag from one season of life to the next. It doesn't matter if we change jobs, move cities, or start over with new people; the backpack follows. Inside are the things we don't talk about: the unprocessed pain, childhood wounds, betrayals we tried to forget, and secrets we promised ourselves we'd take to the grave. It also holds the beliefs we absorbed about who we are and what we deserve, even when those beliefs were never true.

This backpack is filled with the coping mechanisms and survival strategies we once used to protect ourselves. Things that kept us alive but now keep us stuck. We learn to live with the backpack strapped tight, normalizing its weight. We brush off the snapping tone in conversations, the way we shut down when we feel unsafe, or the fact that we stay in places we've long outgrown, never pausing to ask why.

We build relationships with the backpack on. We raise children while carrying it. We chase dreams while pretending it's not there. But the truth is, the backpack is truly never invisible. It shows up in how we love, how we fear rejection, how we avoid vulnerability, and how we silence our own needs. It becomes a shadow companion; uninvited but ever-present.

My emotional backpack was heavy. It was stuffed with unnamed fears, regrets I replayed as late-night reruns, broken dreams collecting dust in the corners of my heart, father wounds I didn't want to admit, people-pleasing that left me drained, and disappointments dressed up as love. I didn't realize how much I was carrying until exhaustion became my normal.

I was drained by relationships that fed on my silence and situations I should've left long ago. I kept whispering to myself: *Just push through. Be strong. Don't make a fuss.* But behind the practiced smile and the "I'm fine" that rolled too easily off my tongue, I was quietly breaking. Breaking in ways no one could see.

My healing didn't begin with some dramatic breakthrough. There was no mountaintop moment, no lightning bolt of clarity. It began with surrender, a small, trembling step toward honesty. It began in therapy, sitting across from a stranger, finally speaking truths I had buried for decades. It continued in quiet conversations with friends where, for the first time, I let myself be seen without a mask. It happened on the living room floor, my body curled into itself, tears spilling faster than I could catch them, words still stuck in my throat. Healing started not with strength, but with finally letting go of the performance of being okay.

Healing, for me, has been anything but pretty; messy, uneven, and full of trial and error. Some days looked like progress: journaling, breathing easier, feeling lighter in my skin. Other days looked like me curled under the covers, convinced I was right back at square one. Healing hasn't been a straight climb toward some mountaintop. It's been a zigzag, a dance between light and shadow, between hope and despair. It's been learning to trust the small shifts: mornings when the weight feels just a little lighter, conversations where my voice doesn't tremble, nights when the silence no longer suffocates.

Here's what I want you to know: healing isn't about perfection, arrival, or becoming someone untouched by pain. Healing is about fragments; the shattered pieces of yourself being gathered, examined, and held with compassion. It's about stitching together wholeness from what was once broken. Healing doesn't erase the past or pretend it never happened. What it does is transform how the past lives inside you. It teaches you that scars are both evidence of survival and symbols of strength.

If you're holding this book, I imagine you've carried your own backpack. Maybe you've learned to hide it so well that people assume you're fine. Maybe you've convinced yourself not to unpack it, that you can keep pushing through. Or maybe, like me, you've reached the point where the straps are digging into your shoulders, and you're simply too tired to carry it anymore. However you arrived here, know this: *you are not alone*. The weight you've been holding doesn't make you weak. It makes you human.

This book won't offer a straight path, a checklist, or a tidy step-by-step. What you'll find here are fragments; pieces of my story, my healing, and the wisdom I've stumbled upon along the way. Some fragments might echo your own story so closely that you feel seen. Others may not resonate, and that's okay. Take what you need, leave the rest. Healing has never been about following someone else's map; it's about learning to trust your own.

I'm not here to offer a formula. Healing isn't linear. It's not one-size-fits-all. I'm simply here to share what helped me unpack my emotional backpack, and maybe help you unzip yours. This isn't about perfection. It's about truth. About what we carry and what we learn to release. It's about breaking cycles, reclaiming your voice, and choosing yourself, even when it's hard. Especially when it's hard.

Here's what I can promise: honesty. I'll tell the truth, even when it's raw, even when it's uncomfortable. I'll share the stories I once wanted to bury, because I believe in breaking the silence. And I'll offer what I've learned, not just as a therapist, but as a woman who has lived through her own wreckage. I know what it's like to feel broken and not know where to begin. If all you can do right now is open this book and breathe, that's enough.

So if you've been carrying your own backpack, tired, pretending, pushing through, waiting for a sign, let this be it. This book is for you. For the woman who whispers *enough* in the middle of the night. For the one who smiles in public and cries in secret. For the one who has carried her pain so long, she's forgotten what freedom feels like. This is for you.

I used to believe the past was gone. Now I understand it was quietly shaping every choice I made.

Chapter 1

The Last Straw

*"All it takes is someone caring enough about you to spark a flame...
then ignite a fire, until you begin to care about you, too."*

Three days after my twenty-eighth birthday, I told myself, enough.
Enough of the cheating.
Enough of the lies.
Enough of the emotional and psychological abuse that had become the backdrop of my life.
What he said to me that day fractured something deep inside me. It was not a movie scene; there was no screaming, no slammed doors. It was quieter and far more defining. A line had been crossed, and I felt it in my body as much as in my heart. It was visceral. I never imagined those words could come from someone who claimed to love me. But they did. And in that moment, I knew I could not take it anymore. That was my last straw.

The day itself gave no warning. My alarm went off at 2 a.m., as always. I washed my face, brushed my teeth, slipped into my uniform, combed my hair, and packed my daughter's things so I could drop her off at my grandmother's before work. Everything felt routine. At the airport, I settled into my ritual: a quick nap in the car before stepping onto the ramp. The sun had not yet risen; the world was still cloaked in darkness, but my mood was light. I was still glowing from my birthday. And if you know me, you know birthdays are sacred. It is the one day I claim as mine, fully and unapologetically.

After finishing my last flight for the morning, I felt relieved; I was getting off early. I gathered my things and headed toward the time clock, ready to start the rest of my day. That's when I saw a missed call from my boyfriend. Odd. He knew I couldn't answer during ramp hours. Curious, I called him back. His voice was casual, almost careless. He said he hadn't eaten and asked if I could bring him lunch. That wasn't unusual; we often shared meals during his breaks. So, without hesitation, I agreed.

I stopped at Popeyes, ordering his favorite: popcorn shrimp, fries, and an Arnold Palmer. A small gesture of love, or at least what I thought was love. When I pulled into the lot at his job, I scanned for his car so I could park beside it, but it wasn't there. My stomach dipped. I dialed his number. No answer. Tried again. Still nothing. Irritation began to rise.

If I had gone out of my way to bring him food and he just vanished without a word, we had a problem. After several more calls, he finally emerged. Even before he opened his mouth, his body language betrayed him: shoulders tight, movements off-kilter, eyes avoiding mine. You know that look when someone is about to lie; the way their entire posture shifts, as if their whole being is trying to hide.

I asked, "Where's your car?"

He paused for a breath, then answered with a hard edge I had learned to read:

"It's my car. I pay the note. I can do whatever I want with it."

That sentence was the first spark, an ember that revealed how dry everything around it had become. He said he had let a female coworker borrow his car to get food. My mind raced. Why was she using his car? If she went to pick up food for him, why hadn't she brought anything back? Why had he called me for lunch if someone else had his keys? None of it added up.

He repeated himself, irritation and arrogance lacing his voice:

"It's my car. I'll let whoever I want to use it. Don't ask me anything about my car; you don't pay any of my bills."

And just like that, something in me snapped.

"You knew I just worked a ten-hour shift. What is wrong with you? Don't act like I'm the problem. Why is another woman driving your car? I don't care if I never paid a single bill; don't disrespect me like that. You called me for food, but she had your keys?"

He didn't look bothered. He snatched the food from my hands and stalked off. Before going inside, he walked to his car. The coworker had returned by then. He reached in, grabbed something, and flung it at me through the open window. It struck my chest and clattered to the car floor. It was my birthday gift, three days late. A watch I had not wanted and had not asked for. Now, I am not the kind of woman who needs grand displays. But when I invest thought and intention into your birthday, when I celebrate you with care, I expect the same in return. This was not care. It felt like a last-minute task checked off someone else's list.

And then, as if a curtain dropped, the whole week slid into view: the days of silence, the missed calls, the hurried dinners, the excuses, the distance. This incident was not a single misstep; it was the punctuation at the end of a pattern.

I got in my car and drove away hollow. I did not have the energy for tears. I had poured time and pieces of myself into him, and this is what I had received. I wanted to scream until my voice broke. I wanted him to feel a fraction of the emptiness I felt. But my pride and my need for peace kept me small and silent.

Still, I wanted answers. I called and called. He ignored me. At last, he picked up and said he would call me on his break. While I waited, I called my friend. The moment she answered, I collapsed. I cried so hard I could not breathe, the kind of sound that comes from deep in the belly and leaves you raw. She listened as I tried to stitch together sense from nonsense.

Eventually, he called back. We circled the same argument. And then he said the words that untied everything.

"You are draining me, physically and mentally."

Seven words that cut deeper than a thousand small betrayals.

The man I loved had just told me, calmly, that I was a burden.

I can't recall exactly what I said back. I remember the collapse of sound in my throat, the way I fell quiet. Heat flooded my skin. My heart plummeted like a stone. I thought of every time I had carried him, shown up, swallowed my pride, and given grace that was not earned, and this was the ledger of my efforts.

A coworker had warned me months before: *If you stay, it will cost you.*

I had not heeded the warning. I told myself I could fix it. I told myself he would change. I told myself love was enough. The warning signs had always been there: small red flags, evasions, those silences that felt louder than words.

I would no longer pretend those were not the truth.

CHAPTER 1: A LOOK BACK

I was done pretending.

I drove straight to my friend's house, the neighborhood lights blurring past like witness marks on the side of the road. Her boyfriend was there when I arrived. The moment I crossed the threshold, words tumbled out of me, half-sobbed, half-ranted, while my hands tried and failed to explain the hollow feeling in my chest.

He listened with that focused silence some people have when they know their words matter. Then, when I faltered, he stopped me mid-sentence and said something I will never forget:

"You deserve better than what you are allowing yourself to have. You did not cause this; he did. He is using you as a dumping ground for everything he refuses to deal with inside himself."

The sentence landed like a mirror. He was right. Even though love still lived somewhere in me for my boyfriend, I had nothing left to offer. My love bank was empty. My soul bank was overdrawn.

When my boyfriend called back later that evening, the part of me that had been flayed open earlier had been bandaged by that small room and two steady listeners. I did not yell. I did not argue. I listened with a strange, new distance, as if I were hearing someone else speak about a stranger. He launched into attacks about my job, my income, my car, my choices, trying to shrink me down with words. And then, like a blow I had been avoiding, realization cut through: *This is who he's always been. This is how he's always seen me.* Not as a partner. Not as a woman to honor. Instead, as someone convenient and never cherished. Replaceable. Disposable.

With a quiet I did not know I had inside me, I said:
"It's over."

Enough was enough. I had been abused, cheated on, dismissed, silenced, and kept hidden in the corners of his life. But now I was done.

When he brought up my daughter, trying to pull at whatever threads of guilt he thought he could use, I wished him well. I told him I would keep praying for him because he clearly needed it, and then I ended the call. The instant the line went dead, something that had been clenched in my chest unclenched. The weight I had hauled around my shoulders for years lifted as if someone had loosened a strap. For the first time in a very long while, I smiled. Not the brittle, practiced smile I wore for others, but a small, honest upturn at the corners of my mouth.

I had just done something I never thought I could do.

I chose me.

When Choosing Yourself Is The Bravest Thing You Can Do

There is a quiet, personal reckoning that finds so many of us. It's the slow, sharp moment when you realize you've been noticed only for what you give, not for who you are. It rarely arrives as a blow. Instead, it comes as an unraveling you feel in your bones. Your hands, once busy with small repairs, go still. Your stomach knots in a way you can't untie. And your voice, trained to smooth and explain, finally cracks when you try to name the hurt.

What makes this moment weighty is the small, immediate fallout. You notice the empty cup you never had time to fill, the photo that no longer matches the woman in the mirror. Then you catch your child's question, the one you do not want them to inherit.

This is not a movie with slamming doors. It is private and absolute. The power is not in drama but in the still, stubborn decision that plants itself under your ribs: *I will not let someone else's appetite shape the edges of my life anymore.* From that small, fierce place, the work of choosing yourself begins; in the way you hold your shoulders, in how you set your boundaries, and in the quiet promises you keep to yourself every day.

The hard truth is this: many of us were taught the wrong lesson, that endurance equals virtue. From house rules and church pews to well-meaning family and clumsy friends, the message was: hold on, pray harder, be patient, make it work, long before anyone taught us to protect our emotional safety. That training leaves gaps. We are not taught how to spot the slow erosion: the way your opinion is minimized, the small humiliations disguised as jokes, the gradual shrinking of your appetite for life. Those micro-wounds accumulate until staying costs more than leaving. And what cuts the deepest is not the breaking but the forgetting; forgetting who you were before you learned to fold your needs into someone else's comfort. Remembering your worth is not sentimental. It is practical, hard work. It asks you to notice the quiet warnings, reclaim the pieces of yourself you surrendered, and name the true cost of what you tolerated in the name of love. That naming begins repair.

I once believed staying proved I was strong, proof I had earned my place. I even wore "staying" like a medal, thinking endurance measured my value. It took time and pain to see that this was a lie that postponed my healing. Endurance without boundaries lets patterns calcify, and staying out of fear, habit, or hope trains your body to accept less while slowly eroding the edges of who you are.

Here's a truth: some people will only love you in ways that require you to disappear. They take what is useful and expect the rest to be folded away. On the surface, it appears to be a partnership, but underneath, it is a survival tactic; a performance you maintain to preserve a peace that is never truly reciprocal. Emotional abuse and chronic devaluation leave measurable harm. People repeatedly exposed to emotional mistreatment are more likely to struggle with depression, anxiety, and persistent stress responses later on, even when physical abuse is absent.[1] [2] That is why staying can cost more than peace; it can cost your health, your clarity, and the possibility of returning to the person you once were.

Choosing to leave that dynamic is not a weakness; it is preservation and reclamation. Choosing yourself isn't selfish, it's sacred. Saying, *I may not have gotten everything right, but I deserve peace*, is not surrender; it is a boundary that protects your body, your mind, and the small future you are trying to build.

So many of us stayed because loneliness felt more dangerous than the slow leak of being unseen. We mistook company for care. That confusion matters because loneliness is not just an unpleasant feeling; it reshapes us. Chronic loneliness changes how the body handles stress; sleep fragments, cortisol rhythms shift, inflammation rises, and the recovery system stays stuck in high alert.[3] [4] [5] Over time, these changes add up to serious health risks.

But the harm isn't only biological; it is also relational. Loving someone and being loved in return are not the same thing. You can pour everything into a person who is never equipped or who refuses to hold you. Not because

---

[1] Abigail Powers, Kerry J. Ressler, and Rebekah G. Bradley, "The protective role of friendship on the effects of childhood abuse and depression," *Depression and Anxiety* 26, no. 1 (October 28, 2008): 46–53, https://doi.org/10.1002/da.20534.

[2] Milen L. Radell et al., "The impact of different types of abuse on depression," *Depression Research and Treatment* 2021 (April 13, 2021): 1–12, https://doi.org/10.1155/2021/6654503.

[3] Anna J Finley and Stacey M Schaefer, "Affective Neuroscience of Loneliness: Potential Mechanisms underlying the Association between Perceived Social Isolation, Health, and Well-Being," *Journal of Psychiatry and Brain Science* 7, no. 6 (January 1, 2022), https://doi.org/10.20900/jpbs.20220011.

[4] Minhal Ahmed, Ivo Cerda, and Molly Maloof, "Breaking the vicious cycle: The interplay between loneliness, metabolic illness, and mental health," *Frontiers in Psychiatry* 14 (March 8, 2023): 1134865, https://doi.org/10.3389/fpsyt.2023.1134865.

[5] Louise C. Hawkley and John T. Cacioppo, "Loneliness Matters: A theoretical and empirical review of consequences and mechanisms," *Annals of Behavioral Medicine* 40, no. 2 (July 21, 2010): 218–27, https://doi.org/10.1007/s12160-010-9210-8.

you are unlovable, but because they value what you give more than who you are. That mismatch looks ordinary until you live inside it: the small acts you do to shrink, the truths you tuck away, the voice you quiet so the peace stays intact. Those adaptations feel useful at first; they keep you safe in the short term. But they teach your nervous system to expect imbalance and your heart to accept less. Repeated emotional neglect and chronic devaluation don't just bruise feelings; they raise the odds of depression, anxiety, and a stress response that becomes your new baseline.[6]

So choosing yourself is both a protest and a repair. It refuses the bargain that your presence will be cheaper than your personhood. It starts by noticing the tiny trade-offs: the kindnesses you withheld from yourself, the boundaries you removed one more time. Then comes practice. Begin with one "no" that honors you. Ask for help directly. Allow one small comfort that reminds your nervous system it is safe. This is not sudden heroism. It is daily loyalty to a new, quieter promise: that peace is not a luxury but a right, and that rebuilding the capacity to be held begins with choosing to hold yourself first.

The "last straw" rarely arrives as a headline-making event. It rarely looks like the dramatic fight people imagine. Often, it is a quiet recalibration inside you, a private, honest re-evaluation of what you will and will not model for the people you love and the person you want to be. It is not the missed birthday or the thrown gift that finally defines it. It is the inner sentence you whisper that reframes everything: *This is not what I want my daughter to see. This is not who I want to be. This is not love.* That sentence is a hinge. It alters how you weigh risk and safety, how you name dignity, and how you imagine your future. It rarely delivers tidy closure. You may still love, grieve, or feel confusion. But that inner shift is catalytic; it is the first deliberate movement toward

---

[6] Veena Kumari, "Emotional Abuse and Neglect: Time to Focus on Prevention and Mental Health Consequences," *The British Journal of Psychiatry* 217, no. 5 (September 7, 2020): 597–99, https://doi.org/10.1192/bjp.2020.154.

reclaiming agency. So, if you are at that edge right now, hear this plainly: Standing your ground is not failure. It is the beginning of real freedom.

You are not weak for leaving a situation that undermines your dignity.

You are not difficult for having needs that require tending.

You are not "too much" for desiring consistency, care, and clarity.

What you are doing is honoring your emotional capacity; choosing to conserve it rather than pour it into a bottomless pit. That choice is not indulgence; it is an act of survival and stewardship. Yes, it will hurt. Yes, you will mourn what might have been, and there will be messy moments. But grief here is compost for growth. With time, your breath will slow, your sleep will begin to restore you, and your laughter will come from a place of truth rather than performance. When you look back, you may feel reverence for the woman who finally said, "no more," because choosing yourself repairs more than the present; it reshapes your future.

What people rarely say out loud is this: emotional abuse doesn't always feel like abuse at first. It doesn't kick the door down; it quiets the room gradually. At first, it looks like miscommunication, a lack of alignment, or the gentle claim that you're "too sensitive." You start to keep score inside your head: *Maybe I'm asking for too much.* Instead of a single violent episode, emotional abuse often takes the form of repeated downgrading: your feelings minimized, your boundaries questioned, your experiences rewritten. Over time, those small acts accumulate into erosion. Your memory of self blurs. Second-guessing becomes reflexive. That's gaslighting: the steady undermining of your reality, not just an argument over dinner.

Here is the clarifying test: love, even when messy, tends toward truth and clarity. People who love you badly still usually tell the truth about what happened. Abuse, by contrast, breeds confusion. It leaves you apologizing for feeling your own pain. That distinction matters because it determines whether your nervous system learns to trust your own sensations, or to outsource that trust to someone who will not keep it safe.

If you find yourself constantly walking on eggshells, policing your tone, or repeatedly explaining simple needs, this is not evidence that you're "too emotional." More than likely, you're under-supported. You're emotionally famished in a place that calls itself love. And here's a truth I hold with conviction: *you will always feel starved in relationships where you're only being fed the bare minimum.* Sometimes we confuse breadcrumbs for meals.

When affection is intermittent, we learn to survive on sporadic gestures, vague promises, or momentary effort, and call it a connection. You adapt by lowering expectations. That adaptation is survival, not flourishing. You stay because it feels safer than the unknown. After all, the fear of being alone convinces you that scarcity is better than nothing. But healing is a process of relearning what real nourishment feels like. It reveals what was always true: *you've been starving all along.* What you're afraid to lose was never feeding you anyway.

I often tell clients that healing from emotional abandonment is like thawing out from frostbite. You've gone numb for so long that when you finally start to feel again, it burns. At first, the sensations are confusing; you may even crave the familiar cold because it once felt safe. That is the paradox of recovery: the thing that hurt you may also have been predictable, and we often prefer predictability to the unknown. The task, then, is to stay. Sit with the discomfort long enough for the nervous system to re-regulate. Keep choosing yourself, even when it feels uncomfortable. Especially when it feels uncomfortable. Because eventually, the warmth does return. Over time, you remember how to trust your instincts. You remember how to sit in your own company and feel whole. You remember how to laugh without waiting for the other shoe to drop.

You learn that your worth isn't up for debate. That your softness isn't a liability. That needing to be seen isn't a flaw; it's human. You learn that boundaries don't make you mean. They make you safe. You learn that "no", a restorative word, can be the most healing word in your vocabulary. And more than anything, you learn that the first time something feels off, you're probably right. Your body knew. Your spirit knew. You just hadn't learned to trust yourself yet. But now you're starting to. And that's where healing begins. That's when the last straw becomes the first step.

Walking away from a relationship that wounded me was one of the hardest things I've ever done, but the ache I carried wasn't only about him. It was about something deeper. When I asked why I had stayed so long, the answer was not only about his shortcomings. It was about patterns I had been rehearsing long before we met. To understand why I stayed, I had to go back. Choosing myself required confronting a deeper script, one I had been avoiding for years: *Why am I always trying to prove I'm worthy of being chosen in the first place?* And that question led me back to the first man who never chose me… my father.

Chapter 2

A Fatherless Daughter

"When a father is missing, the space he leaves behind is not empty. It becomes a quiet ache that teaches a girl to search for herself in places she should never have had to look."

My father lived ten miles away, but on graduation night, the chair with his name on it stayed empty. I kept scanning the bleachers anyway, the way a child scans a crowd for proof she matters. That was the shape of his love for me: close enough to count, far enough to miss. The ache started early, and I learned my body's movements long before I had the words for it. Years later, I would call it what it was, not tragic fate, but a choice. He was here. He simply did not choose presence.

I ached for him in the small, persistent ways that do not make sense to anyone but the child who waits. I watched other little girls curl into their fathers like warm blankets and wondered how to fold myself so I would fit his lap. I wanted the small rituals, the tuck-ins, the whispered reassurances, the fatherly kiss on a scraped knee, that seemed ordinary for everyone else. But those moments were rare for me. I could count the times he showed up on one hand, and the emptiness between those fingers felt louder than any words. That absence reflected at me like a mirror, telling me I was unimportant, that I was accidental. So I stitched my life to that missing piece: every relationship I clung to, every compromise I made, every quiet acceptance of less became a thread tied to him. Over time, the ache changed shape, first raw longing, then a flicker of anger, then the slow calcification of resentment, and finally a cold, hard hate that surprised and frightened me because I knew it could color everything I touched.

He missed so much. He missed scraped knees and birthday candles, the awkward shifts of adolescence when you need someone to say, you're okay, you're not a mistake. He missed the small proofs that stitch a person together: a hand that squeezes your shoulder at a recital, a face in the crowd at graduation that says, I was waiting for you. I walked across stages without that face, and the diplomas in my hands felt like thin paper, proof of survival, yes, but complicated by a void. Even now, years on, the memory makes heat in my chest; I can feel my face flush and my throat tighten as if a crowd is there and I still scan for the one person who never came. Because that's what father wounds do; they don't disappear with time, they live in the body. They live as a stiffness in your neck when someone leaves, as the small, practiced readiness to be let down, as the muscle memory that tightens before you even realize you're bracing. Those wounds are less about dates on a calendar and more about the way your body remembers absence: a pulse that spikes at certain songs, a reflex to apologize when you ask for something simple, the quiet recoil when a door shuts. They are carried like an old bruise, mostly hidden but aching in certain weather, and they wait for language. When you finally name them, the ache doesn't vanish, but it begins to make sense.

Years ago, I decided to try anyway. I wanted answers and closure, to see if the empty spaces could be explained. I reached across the distance to be the bigger person because part of me still wanted a father who would show up for me. That's when the world tilted. I found out through someone else that my grandmother had died two months before, and no one had told me. She had been one of the few in that family who tried, in small ways, to bridge the gap between him and me. The news landed like a question I could not answer. Devastation was immediate, but the deeper fracture came from his reaction. When I called him to ask why I had been kept in the dark, he shrugged responsibility away. He blamed his wife. He said it was her job to tell me. He made me the outsider again in my own family. I remember the sting of that moment vividly: I am your child, I wanted to say. You should have told me, but instead, he gave me excuses. At that point, my life felt shredded: fresh from a car accident, reeling from a breakup, and now this. Another abandonment stacked on top of other losses. I sat on the edge of the phone listening to his words, and then I hung up. I chose distance, the way many wounded people do, cutting contact to protect a raw place inside. Time, though, has a way of softening edges; the sharpness dulls, and the question of whether to try again starts to whisper back in quieter hours.

Eventually, I let the curiosity and the hurt converge and reached out one more time. There was a stubborn child in me that still wanted to be seen, to be accounted for, to hear the explanation that would make sense of years of absence. So I drove to his house unannounced the weekend before Easter, carrying a small peace offering and a heart that felt suspiciously hopeful. The anxiety I felt was not the job-interview kind; it was ancient, body-level fear, palms damp, breath short, pulse bumping against my ribs like an alarm. I kept rehearsing what I would say and how I would hold myself, because part of me wanted to prove I was no longer the frightened little girl. When I walked up to his door, it felt like walking into a room full of strangers, even though it was only him standing on the other side.

When he opened the door, it felt oddly normal to hug someone I had missed so much; the gesture was small and awkward and human. Then I asked the question I had carried for years like a stone: Why weren't you there? You missed graduation, birthdays, the nights I needed someone to say it would be okay. How could you abandon the first person you could have loved without condition, your daughter, the one you passed a look and resemblance to? With so many questions fired in rapid succession, I watched his face for something: remorse, surprise, a splitting regret. Instead, I found what I did not expect: pity. He spoke quickly and blamed his demons: drugs, alcohol, and addiction, words that sounded like confession and yet also like a shield. I wanted to ask the blunt question that sat in my chest: if addiction kept you away from me, why was it not a barrier with my siblings? But I swallowed the question because I wanted to hold myself like armor. I wanted to be the woman who had survived without him. Underneath that armor, though, my child self was there, small, hopeful, wanting explanation and comfort, and I felt her stiffen with every excuse.

For a while, I let myself imagine another kind of relationship. If he could not be the father I needed, maybe he could show up in the smaller, safer role of grandfather to my daughter. I wanted to believe there could be some redemptive arc. I was wrong. The calls started to feel like a new kind of injury: late-night ringings when reason was muffled, and his words were slippery with alcohol. He'd speak in rambling, uneven phrases that felt too intimate, too misplaced. Sometimes the calls left an uneasy taste in my mouth; sometimes they crossed lines that made my skin tighten with shame. Once, he tried to "set me up" with his friends in a way that made my stomach drop. I remember sitting on the bed, phone heavy in my hand, feeling both furious and confused. How could the same man who had vanished when I needed him now be behaving like this? That mix of shame and longing was a bitter, confusing knot. I believed in forgiveness, but forgiveness did not come easily when the wound's hand was the one that had carved it in the first place.

Months passed, and I continued to test the fragile possibility of normalcy. I showed up at holiday tables, practiced the polite, patient smile, and tried on the role of daughter for an audience that had only seen it sporadically. That year, I spent Christmas with him and his family for the first time in my life. I was twenty-six years old. Older than I expected to be when I finally became part of his seasonal scene. We took one family photo, everyone lined up around a couch, my daughter in the bundle, and for a second, the picture looked like the postcards you see in magazines or the "perfect" family. But the photograph felt like an optical illusion. I knew it didn't change the months and years that had come before. Even in that framed moment, I had the strange sensation of being an intruder in a scene I'd been excluded from for decades.

Two and a half years slipped by, and my visits became punctuation marks; rare, awkward, necessary. I saw him twice in that stretch, like a name reappearing on a list. Then his wife, the woman who had done more to bridge our distance than he ever had, died suddenly of a massive heart attack. The irony burned: she had been one of the few who checked on me, who called after my surgery, who offered small kindnesses while he kept his distance. Now she was gone. At the same time, I found myself preparing for another operation, this time for fibroids. Suddenly, the stakes felt higher and the fear more acute. There was the practical possibility that I might lose the chance to have more children. There was the darker possibility that I might not wake up on the surgery table. In the middle of that terror, what I wanted more than anything was human and simple: to see his face, to know, just once, that he noticed me.

When my mother found out, she drove to his house to tell him herself, because mothers do the work of worrying and show up for the children they love into existence. She knocked, and his girlfriend answered, defensive and sharp. When my mother said who she was, the woman barked an order for her to leave and slammed the door. My mother heard his voice somewhere inside the house, faint and distant, but he never crossed the room to the door. Instead, she left a note on his windshield explaining my upcoming surgery and asking him to call. When I heard what had happened, a mixture of fury and grief rose in me. How could he not come to the door? How could he not want to know if I was alive and okay? I drove there myself later that day. The note was still stuffed under the windshield wiper, a humiliating little marker of effort left unacknowledged. I walked up, rang the bell.

Waited.

Knocked.

Waited again.

Still nothing.

So, I finally banged on the door. No one answered. Fifteen minutes passed like an hour. When I left, I ripped the note into pieces and threw them away in the car, the paper fluttering like wasted attempts. I saw one of his friends pull up as I drove off, and I did not stop. I felt myself unraveling, raw in a way that had nothing to do with drama and everything to do with the exhaustion of trying.

That day, something cracked open inside me. I had tried so many times to forgive, to understand, to hope, and still there was no movement from him. It was not a melodramatic severing; it was an exhaustion so absolute that it decided for me. I drew a line not from rage but from the steadiness of necessity. Yes, there was love, complicated and stubborn, but I refused to keep stretching for someone who would not extend his hand back. I stopped begging to be seen and stopped investing energy into fixing what was never mine to fix. The little girl who once prayed for a saving father did not vanish; she was allowed to rest. In her place, a woman rose, tired, resolute, and clear. She chose peace over pain. She stopped seeking closure from the source of the wound. She spoke, silently and finally, the single sentence that had been building inside her for years: *Enough is enough.*

Open Letter To My Father

I have carried this longing for as long as I can remember. I wanted your love in the small, ordinary ways: your attention at the dinner table, your voice calling my name from the other room, your hand on my shoulder when I was scared. I wanted you to see me not only as your child but as someone worth choosing, worth showing up for. Instead, you missed most of it. You missed the slow work of watching me grow into who I would become. You missed my toughest nights and my quiet victories, the times I cried alone and the mornings I stood a little taller. You missed the chance to love a daughter who would have given you everything for a single consistent moment of presence. I expected you to be my protector and my teacher, the model for how a man should love and respect. You weren't there to teach me that. You weren't there to warn me away from men who would hurt me. You weren't there when I turned on the light to face my reflection and asked myself, Why am I not enough? So I began to look in the same places I had seen before, faces that echoed yours, gestures that felt familiar, and I tried to buy the affection I needed. I worked to earn attention, to hold people with words and chores and patience, because I had never been shown what being loved without condition actually feels like.

I sometimes pull out the only photo we have together and hold it like evidence of a life that might have been. I imagine a different thread of my story, one where your presence taught me steadiness, not absence. Would I have walked into rooms with less hesitation? Would I have trusted sooner, loved more wisely? Those are unanswerable questions, and they hover like ghosts. That little girl, imagined as safe because a father was there, will always exist in the shadow of what could have been. But I don't live there now. I live in the real part of my life: the messy, brave, imperfect life I built without you. I keep the photo not as a wound but as a marker, a thing that names a loss but does not decide my worth.

Over time, I learned something important: I don't need your explanations to be whole. I don't need an apology that might never come or a dramatic reunion staged to soothe old wounds. I stopped holding my life hostage to the hope that you would become the man I needed. Healing doesn't require your permission. Peace doesn't always arrive wrapped in closure. Sometimes peace is the quiet decision to stop reaching for what was never offered. It is choosing to stop circling the same question and instead, build a life that does not hinge on your recognition.

Your absence became, painfully and strangely, a teacher. It taught me, by contrast, how to show up for my child in the ways I had been denied. I learned to love with steadiness, to answer the late-night tears, to celebrate small victories with consistent presence. It made me intentional about the rhythms of care I provide and focused on protecting the small, ordinary moments that become a child's sense of safety. While I would have preferred a different lesson, one learned through your presence, I accept the purpose that emerged anyway. For that, strangely, I am thankful: not for what you gave, but for what your absence forced me to become. I am strong not because you made me so, but despite what you couldn't offer. I pray, quietly, that someday you will find peace and the courage to forgive yourself. But whether that happens or not, I am moving forward, not angrily, not bitterly, but free.

For the little girl I protected, free with gratitude,
A Fatherless Daughter

No More Waiting At The Door

There is a wound that never shows up on an X-ray but still leaves a physical signature: a tremor in your voice, a smile that sits too tight, the small instinctive brace you take when someone reaches for your hand. It is not imaginary; it is embodied. When a father is physically present but emotionally absent, his absence is learned by your nervous system as a kind of truth about who you are and how the world will treat you. That lesson does not only live in memory; it lives in posture, in sleep patterns, and in the reflex to expect withdrawal before it happens. Over time, those patterns shape the person you become, the ways you love, the ways you guard, and the ways you measure worth.

We don't talk enough about this kind of grief the way we name other losses, so we don't get the rituals or permission that help us process pain. There is no graveside, no program, no single night where you close a door and move on. Instead, there is the long buildup of missed chances and muffled apologies. That uncertainty keeps you stuck in hope. You tell yourself this will be the visit, the call, the holiday that changes everything. When those openings don't come, waiting hardens into a prison of deferred life. Liberation rarely arrives when the absent person finally returns. Freedom comes when you stop expecting their return to do the work of your repair and instead release yourself to build the life that needs you to be whole.

When a father is absent, physically, emotionally, or spiritually, it doesn't just leave a hole; it teaches. It scripts your internal world with messages you didn't choose but learned to live by:

"You are too much."
"Your needs are a burden."
"Love must be earned."
"Presence is optional."
"Safety is negotiable."

Unless that script is confronted, it becomes the foundation for how you date, how you attach, how you parent, and how you view yourself when no one's watching. Absence doesn't simply subtract; it rewrites the rules you live by. The child who grows up without a reliable paternal presence internalizes a set of beliefs, often unspoken, that become default operating rules for adulthood.[7] [8] Those rules tell you that your wants are indulgences, that affection is earned, and that safety is conditional. These internal scripts organize attachment behaviors: some people become hypervigilant and anxious, always seeking confirmation; others learn to avoid closeness to protect themselves from anticipated rejection.[9] The architecture of these patterns is described by attachment theory, which explains how early caregiving shapes internal working models of self and other, and it helps explain why a missing caregiver can echo through dating, parenting, and self-worth unless deliberately

---

[7] Angus G. Craig et al., "The Long-term Effects of Early Paternal Presence on Children's Behavior," *Journal of Child and Family Studies* 27, no. 11 (August 20, 2018): 3544–53, https://doi.org/10.1007/s10826-018-1206-1.

[8] Sara McLanahan, Laura Tach, and Daniel Schneider, "The Causal Effects of Father Absence," *Annual Review of Sociology* 39, no. 1 (July 19, 2013): 399–427, https://doi.org/10.1146/annurev-soc-071312-145704.

[9] Brown, Whitney. "Shattered Innocence, Scarred Love: A Phenomenological Study on the Effects of Childhood Sexual Abuse of African American Women on their Romantic Relationships." Order No. 31937022, University of Holy Cross, 2025. https://uhcno.idm.oclc.org/login?url=https://www.proquest.com/dissertations-theses/shattered-innocence-scarred-love-phenomenological/docview/3201918934/se-2.

addressed in therapy or relational repair.[10] [11] That's the unspoken power of a father wound: it echoes long after the silence.

When presence was unreliable growing up, the practical adaptations you learned to survive, people-pleasing, overworking, caretaking, become habits that look like competence on the surface but are actually compensations for unmet needs. You become an expert at reading other people's moods while losing the ability to notice your own. This hyper-responsiveness helps keep relationships functional in the short term, but it trains your system to accept intermittent reinforcement, those small, unpredictable rewards that keep behavior repeating. Neuroscience shows this pattern is powerful. That's why so many of us mistake chemistry for bond, proximity for safety, and infrequent kindness for love, because it feels like home. Then we wonder why peace is foreign.

We don't just feel unloved; we begin to feel unlovable. That distinction changes everything, which is why naming the wound matters. When unlovability becomes a story you tell about yourself, it paints choices, who you invite close, how you talk to your children, and how long you remain in harmful situations. Naming the wound helps dissolve that narrative because names create distance. Once something is named, it can be observed and worked on rather than endured. This process, naming, mapping, and then practicing new relational behaviors, is the core of healing. It is how you replace old scripts with new patterns of safety, reciprocity, and self-respect.

---

[10] Colleen Doyle and Dante Cicchetti, "From the Cradle to the Grave: The Effect of Adverse Caregiving Environments on Attachment and Relationships Throughout the Lifespan.," *Clinical Psychology Science and Practice* 24, no. 2 (April 11, 2017): 203–17, https://doi.org/10.1111/cpsp.12192.

[11] John Bowlby and Tavistock Institute of Human Relations, *Attachment and Loss*, Basic Books, Second Edition, vol. I (Basic Books, 1982), https://mindsplain.com/wp-content/uploads/2020/08/ATTACHMENT_AND_LOSS_VOLUME_I_ATTACHMENT.pdf.

Holding two truths at once is essential here: fathers are people with histories, and their failures can still wound deeply. Trauma, addiction, and neglect can explain patterns of absence, but explanation is not absolution; it doesn't erase the harm. You can acknowledge someone's humanity while still grieving what you deserved.

You should have had more. You should have had someone who celebrated your birthdays, clapped at your school performances, and showed up for your heartbreaks. Someone who warned you about the world, modeled protection, and affirmed your beauty before it was ever questioned. When you don't get that, you go looking for it. Of course you do. The heart seeks continuity. If your earliest model of love is intermittent or conditional, you'll unconsciously scan for echoes of that pattern in partners, even when those partners are just as unavailable. That tendency is survival, an attempt to make the world familiar and therefore predictable. But survival is not the same as healing. Healing means learning to choose differently, to practice new models of reciprocity and consistency rather than replaying old scripts.

Healing looks less like a dramatic cure and more like a quiet reorientation of daily life: stop performing for love, stop tuning your moods to fit someone else, and let yourself begin to receive. It's the moment you stop knocking at locked doors and instead start building rooms where you are already welcomed. That doesn't mean you'll never be triggered again. Trauma leaves markers, sensations, and memories that still surface. The difference is that those triggers no longer hijack your decisions. You learn to notice them, name them, and choose despite them. That shift from reactive survival to intentional response is the work of healing, and it is practical.

If peace ever comes, it won't arrive through a dramatic apology or a long-overdue reunion. More often, it arrives modestly: in the quiet mornings you spend not rehearsing how to be lovable but simply being comfortable in your own skin. Peace is not erasure of memory; it is memory re-held without being contaminated by shame. It is the act of setting down emotional baggage that was never yours to carry and saying plainly, I deserve calm, safety, and respect, even if I never receive them from you. That claim is hard because many of us, women with father wounds, were socialized to chase approval and earn belonging. But peace is not a prize you win by endurance; it is a right you reclaim through practice. Relearning that you are whole despite absence is the first concrete step back to yourself.

Wanting to be "daddy's girl" is not childish; it is human. Children expect protection from caregivers, and that expectation is a biological necessity. When that protection is absent, the sensible response is to become your own guardian. Protecting yourself doesn't mean constructing armor that isolates you; it means erecting boundaries that preserve your safety, speaking truth to reset relational expectations, and practicing self-compassion so your worth does not wobble with another person's attention. Those are active, skillful choices, daily habits that rewire how you relate. They are the opposite of resignation: they are insistence, practiced quietly every time you choose a healthy boundary over a familiar compromise.

There is something sacred in that moment of elective self-parenting, when you stop expecting an absent parent to transform and instead choose to teach, steady, and hold yourself. It is not bitterness; it is dignity. It is not cold detachment; it is careful care. That transformation is the work of repair. You step into a role you once longed to be given and, in doing so, you model love for yourself and for the children in your life. Building your days with intentional tenderness, setting limits that protect your margins, and practicing small acts of presence for yourself, these are not substitutes for what you missed; they are the new architecture of a life healed enough to flourish. Those are the moments the little girl stops waiting and begins creating her own life, with her own hands.

So if you're still holding out for the apology, the letter, the sudden realization that he finally understands, permit yourself to stop. Waiting is a strategy that once kept you safe. It no longer serves the life you want. Permit the grief to come. That grief is testimony that something mattered. At the same time, permit yourself to build. It helps illustrate that recovery can include real, meaningful change. You are not irreparably broken, and your chance to be loved is not past. The most radical, generative act is choosing yourself. Letting go of the script that your worth depends on another's recognition and instead living as the person who recognizes and protects you. When you do that, you do not leave hollow; you leave transformed, ready to receive reciprocity rather than chase it.

But What Does Moving On Really Look Like?

We often misread healing as the disappearance of pain, as if becoming healed means never feeling the ache again. In therapy, I have learned something different. Healing is not the absence of the wound. It is the ability to carry the wound without letting it dictate who you become and the choices you make. Moving on does not annul what happened; it removes the past from the place of authority in your story.

The work starts with naming. Not a private, wishful denial, but a clear naming. Start here and ask yourself:
- What did he not give, and how did that absence steer your behavior?
- How did my first lessons about love teach me to prioritize performance over presence?
- Which patterns entered my life as survival moves and stayed as habits?

If you refuse to name these things, they remain on autopilot, running your life.

CHAPTER 2: A FATHERLESS DAUGHTER

Healing cannot root in denial. So name the injuries. Name the person who caused them when you can. Name the ache. Then keep going and name the truths you have been avoiding. Speak aloud the sentences you have practiced inside your head for years. Say them and let them sound true and small:

- I tried to be enough for people who didn't have a model for what was enough.
- I've avoided vulnerability because I learned that emotional neediness leads to rejection.
- I've confused inconsistency with chemistry because abandonment was my first blueprint.

Naming doesn't undo the past, but it clears the soil for mourning. Once you name the truth, you stop mistaking phantom hope for real repair. Naming is preparation. It is the map you need before you start to mourn.

Grief here is complicated because what you are grieving is partly imaginary and partly real. You grieve not only what happened but also the tender image you built to survive: the father who would meet you, hold you, and steady you. Letting go of that fantasy is not a betrayal of love. It is a necessary unhooking. That mourning can feel like a small death, but there is a vital emergence on the other side. When grief has room to move through you, it clears out false expectations and makes space for self-parenting, the deliberate practice of giving yourself the care you never received.

The real work is not a dramatic rebirth. It is the small, almost invisible practice of tending to yourself in ordinary moments. Healing happens on Tuesday afternoons, in the bedside rituals, in the sentences you say when no one else is listening. Start by asking the questions and then answering them on your own:

- What would the steady, loving father say to me today?
- What would he have said the night I failed, or the morning I made a small victory?

Then speak those sentences to yourself with kindness. That is reparenting: you become the steady voice that once waited at the window. As you do this, you begin to test the beliefs that were handed to you by absence. You interrogate them rather than inherit them. Ask yourself:
- Do I still operate like love is something I must earn?
- Do I reduce my worth to what I provide?

Then answer them aloud. Those questions begin the emotional retraining, the rewiring of a nervous system that learned to brace for disappointment. You learn how to stay present when someone offers you care without a catch. You stop apologizing for existing. You learn how to breathe again in spaces that feel unfamiliar because they're healthy. Then the practice begins. You practice boundaries, not to punish others, but to protect yourself. You stop explaining your worth. You stop personalizing people's inability to love you properly. You learn that someone's limits are not your responsibility; they never were. Slowly, your pattern of attraction changes. You stop chasing emotionally unavailable people. You stop calling it fate when it's familiarity. You start seeking softness instead of spark. Safety instead of suspense. You choose peace, even if it feels boring at first, because you understand now that calm is not emptiness. It's security. It's your nervous system finally saying, I'm safe.

Moving on is not always the cinematic exit scene. Often it is discreet and private: you unfollow the illusion, delete the late-night number, and let the grief come in therapy. You write letters you will never send to make sense of your history. Sometimes the bravest act is not a great speech but the steady decision to stop performing to prove your worth. That choice does not erase who you are; it reveals more of you, your real self, by removing what never belonged to you.

So, if you're still asking how to move on, the answer is simple and practical: make small, deliberate choices. Each time you choose honesty instead of fantasy, say no to the pattern and yes to a boundary, choose to be present with yourself rather than vanish into someone else's life, you are moving. The burden will linger at times, but it becomes shared with trusted people, with practices, and with self-care rather than carried as a secret alone. You place the weight down brick by brick and build something new on the rubble; an imperfect, steady life that belongs to you. That life isn't lesser for being repaired, it is more you. You are no longer the child at the door. You are the woman who turned away, palms empty but ready, able finally to receive what you have always deserved.

Therapist's Work For The Reader: For The Fatherless Daughter

You do not need closure from him to begin reclaiming your life. What you need is clarity and small, repeatable practices that teach your body and mind that you are safe to receive. His absence shaped parts of you, that's true, but it does not get to write your ending. Choosing your ending starts with naming what was missing and giving yourself the care that fills the gap. Below is a short exercise, an immediate script, and a tiny plan you can follow this week. Do them in order. Each one is a step toward practical freedom.

10–15 minute naming & release exercise (do this first)

1. Find a quiet place. Set a timer for 10 minutes.
2. Close your eyes for a slow breath in and out three times. Open your journal. Write, without editing, the moment you remember waiting for him, and he didn't show. Keep the details simple (time, place, what you needed).

3. Answer these aloud, one after the other (speak to the younger you):

   - What did I need in that moment?
   - What did I tell myself it meant when he wasn't there?
   - What would I say to myself now, knowing what I know?

4. When the timer ends, tear up (or ceremonially fold) that page and put it away. This physical gesture signals release. (If tearing is too much, put the page in a folder labeled Release.)

A script you can say now (use as a mirror practice).

Look at yourself and say:

- "I see you. You did the best you could. You deserved protection, care, and a steady presence. I will give you what was missing."

Repeat this aloud for 1–3 minutes each day this week.

Mini 1-week plan (small, doable steps)

- **Day 1 (Naming):** Do the 10–15 minute exercise above.
- **Day 3 (Reparenting script):** Say the mirror script morning and night. Write one short sentence to your younger self and keep it in your wallet/phone.
- **Day 7 (Boundary trial):** Choose one small boundary to practice (e.g., don't answer a call after 9 p.m.; say "I can't right now" instead of overexplaining). Notice how your body responds.

Reflection prompts (5–10 minutes)

- What changed after I said the mirror script once? Three days? A week?
- Which boundary felt doable? Which felt hard? Why?
- Who can I tell about this week's work so I'm not doing it alone?

Micro-practices that build safety

- Two-minute grounding: 4–4–8 breath (inhale 4, hold 4, exhale 8). Repeat 4 times when anxiety spikes.
- Reparenting phrase bank: "You were seen. You are safe now." / "It wasn't your fault." / "I will protect you." Pick one, say it quietly to yourself when fear rises.
- Boundary script (2 lines): "I appreciate you, but I can't engage in that right now." No explanation necessary.

Why does this work?

Naming interrupts autopilot. Speaking the truth aloud engages the body (not just the mind) and begins to rewire responses. Practicing small boundaries teaches your nervous system that safety can be predictable. These are not magic cures; they are steady, brain-and-body-based steps toward reclaiming agency.

Homework (do this each week for a month)

1. One naming exercise (10–15 min).
2. Daily mirror script (1–3 min).
3. One boundary is practiced publicly or privately.
4. Brief weekly check-in: write one sentence about progress ("This week I noticed…").

A closing permission:

You do not need his permission to heal. You do not need his apology to be whole. Start here, with the small, daily practices that return you to yourself. I'll walk with you through the next section, where we translate these habits into longer-term change.

Fatherlessness teaches you how to pretend to be whole long before you even understand what is missing.

When something essential is missing early, the wound is not the absence itself, but what the child learns to carry in its place.

Chapter 3

Bruised Soul

"A bruised soul is born long before the bruise is ever seen. It begins the moment a child realizes her home is not a place where love protects but a place where fear teaches her how to survive."

No child imagines her life will be defined by surviving. We dream of futures painted in bright colors, weddings, first apartments, laughter echoing through kitchens, not a life where affection leaves bruises or love must be measured by the weight of silence. I didn't plan to learn invisibility as a skill. But that's what happens when your earliest lessons come from watching someone you love flinch before a blow. My mother taught me endurance, though she never meant to. Witnessing her pain was supposed to be a warning. Instead, it became a map, tucked into the edges of every choice I made. Trauma is patient, seeping in quietly, shaping who we become long before we realize what it's done. I learned how a raised voice rearranges the air in a room. How laughter becomes rationed. How a child learns to gauge danger by the way adults stand. That was my classroom, my education in survival.

My mother was made of quiet strength. She didn't wear resilience like armor; it was closer to breath, woven into the way she moved through a room. But that strength came at a cost. Each day demanded small sacrifices: folding her dreams smaller, tucking away her opinions, exchanging her own softness for safety. The men she loved mistook that self-preservation for permission. They called their control "protection" and tightened their grip until the air itself felt monitored. Watching her live like that taught me that love required endurance, that safety was earned by silence. I didn't yet understand that her survival wasn't a weakness; it was a strategy. But I also didn't see how much of herself it cost her to stay alive in those rooms.

One boyfriend came home smelling of cheap beer. The apartment changed the moment his key turned in the lock. The air went heavy. The stove clock slowed its tick. Tension collected in the corners, like static before thunder. When the door opened, ordinary things sharpened: a clink of silverware felt like accusation, a laugh like defiance, a cooling plate evidence of disrespect. He moved through our kitchen with the entitlement of a man who thought rules bent for him. If something in the house displeased him, a meal not hot enough, a tone too sharp, a glance too long. His voice thundered, doors slammed, and threats flew like thrown objects. Sometimes my mother answered back, her words cutting through the air like a small act of rebellion. But most nights, she folded inward, the way a bird tucks its wings to survive the shadow of a hawk.

I remember the night everything changed. I was eight, lying beneath my sheets, when the crash came, a sharp shatter that broke through the dark. Then her scream. The sound was so pure, so sharp, it carved a new place in me. I ran into the kitchen and found our dinner ruined and her on the floor, blood bright against her lip. He stood over her, breathing hard. My instinct was to scream, to hit, to throw something. But children in homes like that learn early that noise doesn't stop the violence; it invites it closer.

She rose slowly, like someone navigating broken glass, hand trembling as she touched her own blood. "Go back to bed," she whispered, voice calm in the way only mothers can be when they are bleeding and still trying to protect their child. That was what broke me most, her apology in the middle of her pain. I went back to my room, not because anything was all right, but because staying meant danger. That was the first time I remember feeling completely powerless.

He wasn't the only one. He was part of a pattern. Faces changed, excuses shifted, but the choreography stayed the same: flirtation, control, explosion, apology. Repetition becomes its own kind of truth. When something happens enough times, it begins to feel inevitable. Another man came at her with a knife. His pacing filled the hallway, his rage swallowed the house. My mother tried to hold the moment steady, but her fear was visible, trembling at the edges of her control. I watched from the crack of my bedroom door, praying he wouldn't notice me. He didn't. That was mercy enough. When it was over, things were broken again, but she was alive. Survival felt fragile, like a coin toss you hope lands your way.

Another time, he grabbed her by the hair and dragged her down the hall. I screamed until my throat burned and my ribs ached. People heard. I know they did. Windows closed. Footsteps paused. But no one came. It wasn't just the violence that hurt; it was the silence around it. That was the night I learned that help doesn't always come, and that lesson taught me how to make myself smaller.

Life in that apartment became a slow erosion, her laughter less frequent, her movements cautious, her voice measured. She learned to edit herself to survive. I learned to perform normally at school, smiling on command, never mentioning what waited at home. Silence became our second language, one that kept us safe but also stole our freedom. You learn, in homes like that, to exist without drawing attention, to hold your breath until the danger passes. But childhood shouldn't be about holding your breath.

Children remember what they see, even when they can't explain it. And I remembered everything. The fear. The apologies. The pretending. That house stole more than my safety; it rewrote my definition of love. No one tells you that witnessing abuse is its own kind of trauma. The bruises may not have shown on my skin, but they bloomed inside me, on my mind, my sense of worth, my understanding of affection. Those invisible bruises followed me into womanhood, whispering lies that sounded like truth: *This is just what love is. This is passion. This is normal.* But it wasn't normal. It was survival. It was pain dressed up as devotion.

I swore I would never repeat her story. I told myself no one would ever touch me like that, not my body, not my child, not my life. The vow was sincere. But trauma doesn't respect vows; it recreates what it knows. When you grow up in chaos, your nervous system learns to crave it. You start confusing control with care, volatility with passion. I thought strength alone could protect me. I was wrong. I didn't see the trap because I assumed strength would protect me. Strength alone is not the same as a healthy example. Strength without healing just makes you strong enough to stay in harm's way longer.

My first encounter with abuse in my own life came when I was seventeen, my daughter only six months old. I invited her father to talk, hoping his presence could repair what words had broken. The argument escalated quickly. When he moved to leave, I stepped into the doorway, desperate to stop the unraveling. That desperation wasn't love; it was fear. A fear I had inherited. I tell this not to justify, but to illuminate how old patterns disguise themselves as instinct.

And let me pause here, because this matters:

If a man is determined to go, step aside and let the door close. Blocking his exit, pleading, trying to make him stay, those reactions are born from fear, not love. I learned that begging could turn danger into disaster. Sometimes the closed door is mercy wearing ordinary clothes. That lesson cost me dearly, but it saved my life later.

Back to that night.

He shoved me so hard I hit the refrigerator. The metal slammed cold against my back as I clutched my baby. If the fridge hadn't stopped me, we both would've hit the floor. Betrayal hit harder than the impact. I set my daughter down, adrenaline rising, anger blurring logic. I chased him into the street, fueled by memories of my mother on the kitchen floor, of promises I'd made never to become her. I wanted justice, or something that felt like it. We clashed in the street. He wrapped his arms around me, a bear hug that became a trap, squeezing until my lungs gave out. My world narrowed to sound and light. In that brute squeeze, a single, desperate act of survival pushed through me, and I bit him. I bit until I tasted blood and felt his body recoil. He dropped me and bolted. I gave chase. Adrenaline made my legs keep up. My brother appeared from the house and took up the pursuit. We rounded a corner together, and everything shifted: a gun. I don't know where it came from, I only know how it looked: black, small, final. My brother's shout cut through the night, "He's got a gun! Run!" I ran as if the sound of my own feet could be louder than that single mechanical click that followed. I ran for my daughter, for my mother, for a future I hadn't even imagined yet. The shot went off behind me, a noise that seemed to both matter and not matter because the priority was to move. The sound was muffled, but unmistakable. The shot that followed didn't find me, but it could have.

That night, I learned how thin the line is between life and death, and how easily love can turn into danger.

The thought of not being there to raise my daughter haunted me. The idea that my mother might bury me, me, her daughter who swore to do better, was unbearable. And for what? A man who turned his pain into power, who called violence "love"? At seventeen, I learned a new identity: the girl who had almost died for love. Trauma doesn't just hand you wisdom; it hands you confusion, shame, and the ache of unfinished survival.

I didn't leave that moment feeling stronger in the way people imagine survivors become strong. I left it more broken, more muddled about where responsibility lived and how to keep myself safe. The pattern didn't end there. Abuse returned in quieter disguises: manipulation masquerading as concern, control dressed as care. I told myself endurance was strength, that patience could heal. But survival isn't strength; it's just staying alive. Healing is what turns survival into freedom, and I wasn't free yet.

For years, I clung to a false narrative: that endurance was proof of strength. That if I endured, defended, and survived, I was winning. But survival isn't just strength; it's just survival. I didn't need to keep surviving. I needed to be healed. That truth took time to reveal itself to me. For a long time, I convinced myself that love meant self-erasure. I thought if I became softer, calmer, more forgiving, they would finally change. They never did. I kept trying to save people who didn't want to be saved, mistaking my desperation for devotion. What I thought was courage was really the stubborn repetition of an old script: love requires sacrifice. Two wounded people can't heal each other simply because they want to. And my attempts to save others were not noble rescues; they were codependent bargains where I paid with my safety. I realized then that I was addicted to the idea of saving people. Unlearning that belief would be the real work to come.

I could have died that night. No milestones, no laughter, no future for my daughter. Just silence. I think of that often, the thin line between the life I live now and the life that might have ended on a street at seventeen. I share this not to sensationalize my pain, but to reach the one who still believes that if she just loves harder, he'll change. You don't need another bruise to prove it's abuse. You don't owe explanations to people who refuse to see your worth. You deserve safety, without conditions, without apology. If you see yourself in these words, don't wait. Leaving is not a weakness. It is survival. It is self-respect. It is a legacy.

This Is Not Normal

Some wounds don't leave visible marks. They show up instead in how your body reacts to touch, how your voice tightens, and how carefully you measure safety. That is the residue of intimate partner violence. The physical injuries are reshaping not only your body, but also your belief systems about love and danger. Research tells part of the story: millions of women experience physical, sexual, or psychological violence from a partner in their lifetime. These population figures rise further when non-physical abuse, coercion, control, and persistent humiliation are counted, and experts caution that some groups (including many women of color) are underrepresented in reporting because of stigma, surveillance, and barriers to disclosure. Yet, these statistics can't measure the silence, the way fear hides behind makeup or laughter, the way children learn to gauge danger by listening for footsteps. The numbers are not abstract. They live in neighborhoods, in classrooms, in women who still ask, Was it bad enough to count? So, let me say this clearly:

If it made you question your worth or safety, it counts.
If it made you question your sanity, it counts.

If you had to hide it, explain it away, or beg someone to see you, it counts.

Abuse doesn't always begin with a black eye. Sometimes, it begins with control: what you wear, who you talk to, how much you laugh. It whispers, *you're too sensitive*, *you're overreacting*, or *you're imagining things*, until one day, you no longer recognize yourself. You don't move without scanning the room for how they'll respond. You start apologizing for existing. This pattern often starts early.

Children who grow up in these homes often internalize chaos as normalcy. Neuroscience confirms what survivors know intuitively: prolonged exposure to threat changes the brain.[12] The amygdala, our internal alarm, becomes hypervigilant. Cortisol floods the system. Your body learns to live on the blueprint you created. You grow into adulthood feeling safest in chaos, not because you want it, but because your body expects it. You trust inconsistency. You mistake anxiety for chemistry. You flinch emotionally even when no one raises their voice. You apologize for things that aren't your fault. You stay longer than you should. You convince yourself that pain is love because pain feels familiar. But let me say it again: this is not normal. It never was. Love should not make you afraid. It shouldn't leave you hiding bruises, nor isolate you, humiliate you, or distort your reality. Real love does not require pain to prove it is real. That is why survivors can be baffled by their own responses. The body remembers what the conscious mind tries to forget. That conditioning doesn't dissolve overnight; it's something you slowly untangle with tools, practice, and time.

Healing is not quick work. It's slow, deliberate, and sacred, the steady retraining of your body to trust peace again. It's teaching your mind that calm is not the same as boredom and letting your nervous system know it's safe to

---

[12] J. Douglas Bremner, "Traumatic Stress: Effects on the Brain," *Dialogues in Clinical Neuroscience* 8, no. 4 (December 31, 2006): 445–61, https://doi.org/10.31887/dcns.2006.8.4/jbremner.

rest. Healing begins in small, measurable ways: learning to tolerate quiet without panic, to sit in calm without explaining yourself, to notice when your body no longer braces for the next storm. These are learned capacities, not moral failures. What you once called "keeping the peace" was survival. Now, the work is to replace survival patterns with ones that sustain you.

Healing also means reintroducing yourself to a version of safety that isn't performative. It's understanding that the person who hurt you is not your mirror. You are not their words. You are not their shame, their blame, or their violence. You are someone who adapted to danger, and now, you are learning to live without it. This process will test you. It will ask you to revisit the memories you've buried and face the reasons you stayed. You'll grieve not only the relationship, but the fantasy of who you hoped they would become. But with time, therapy, support, and truth, you will rebuild. You will start to recognize love that doesn't make you small. You'll learn to trust silence, not because someone is holding back rage, but because the room is finally calm. You'll learn to hold peace without flinching, to feel safe without having to earn it, explain it, or fight for it

Healing is not linear. Some days will feel like backsliding, and that is normal. Some days you'll wonder if you made it all up; you didn't. Abuse confuses; healing clarifies. The longer you stay committed to your clarity, the more whole you become. You don't owe anyone your pain story. But if you choose to share it, let it be a light, not a wound. Let it testify, not to how broken you were, but to how resilient you are. And maybe, just maybe, someone else will see your story and believe in their own.

The bruise wasn't visible, but it changed how heavy everything felt.

Chapter 4

The Blues

"What makes depression so heavy is not sadness, but the absence of hope. It is the feeling that even rest will not restore what has been taken."

Depression didn't begin in my adulthood; it settled in early, quiet as dusk. Long before I had language for it, it was already there, sitting beside me at eight years old in the room I shared with my sister. I didn't know what to call the heaviness. I just knew I didn't feel like the other kids. I cried for reasons I couldn't name. I prayed to disappear often. And even then, I believed something was wrong with me.

Clinically, depression refers to a mood disorder marked by ongoing emotional distress, diminished interest or pleasure in activities, and impairment in social, occupational, or personal functioning.[13] But if you've lived it, you know it's more than that. It's a shadow that colors everything: how you move through the world, how you see yourself, how you imagine your future. Depression doesn't always scream; sometimes it just leaves. It drains you of sound, of color, of connection, until all that's left is the echo of what used to be joy.

In their article published through the Centers for Disease Control and Prevention, McGee and Thompson report that approximately one in ten Americans experiences depression, with higher rates observed among young adults between 18 and 25 years old, individuals who are unemployed, and those who lack health insurance.[14] But I was just a little Black girl, barely eight years old, not even close to fitting those categories. I wasn't a young adult, divorced, or uneducated. I was just a child. The only box I checked was *being Black*.

While I didn't know what depression was, I knew what sadness felt like. Because in my world, we didn't talk about mental health. Not at school. Not at church. Not at home. If you were sad, you prayed. If you were tired, you slept. If you were broken, you buried it. So I buried it.

And then the night came that split my childhood in half.

My mom's boyfriend had been around a while. He was no stranger to anger, and we'd already seen the damage his hands could do. During the day, his violence was loud and predictable. But at night, it became something else, quieter, darker, deliberate. One night, he entered our room while we were sleeping. I never slept deeply, so when I heard his

---

[13] "Depression (Major Depressive Disorder) - Symptoms and Causes," Mayo Clinic, n.d., https://www.mayoclinic.org/diseases-conditions/depression/symptoms-causes/syc-20356007.

[14] Robin E. McGee and Nancy J. Thompson, "Unemployment and Depression Among Emerging Adults in 12 States, Behavioral Risk Factor Surveillance System, 2010," *Preventing Chronic Disease* 12 (March 13, 2015): E38, https://doi.org/10.5888/pcd12.140451.

footsteps, I stilled my breath and pretended to sleep. He walked to the window, staring out as if something called to him. But something about his stillness felt wrong. Then I felt it, his hand brushing my leg, moving higher. I froze. I was eight. I didn't have words for what was happening, but I knew it was wrong. I prayed silently, "God, please stop this. Please let me disappear." Something inside me said move. When I shifted, he pulled away, mumbled something about checking the window, and walked out.

But the damage had already begun.

A few nights later, he came back. This time, he didn't stop. That night, he didn't just touch me, he took something from me. My safety. My voice. My trust in the dark. He became both the monster in my nightmares and the man who smiled across the breakfast table the next morning. During the day, he was violent. At night, he was something worse. And I said nothing. Because who would believe me? I was a child. He was *family*.

In our home, silence was the price of survival. We didn't talk about depression, molestation, or suicidal thoughts. We just kept it moving. So I did too. I kept moving, pretending, breathing quietly through the ache. But inside, I was unraveling. I couldn't sleep without the lights on. Couldn't walk down the hall without holding my breath. Every creak of the house made my body tense. I learned to study the shadows under the door, watching for the flicker of movement, the pause that meant danger was coming.

I started sleeping in layers, hoodies, jeans, anything thick enough to make it harder for him to reach me. I'd lie there drenched in sweat, pretending I was just cold. I kept clothes under my pillow, ready to make a quick escape. I even tried barricading the door once with chairs, thinking that it would work. Eight years old, engineering my own safety plan in a house that refused to admit I needed one.

My sister slept across from me, unaware. I don't blame her. She was a child, too. But I remember staring at her in the dark, wondering why it was me. Why my bed? Why my body? I tried switching beds once to confuse him. That night, he didn't come. But the next night, he did. Somehow, he knew. Like fear left a scent. Like my silence had its own signal.

I began to prefer school to home, not because I loved learning, but because it was the only place *he* wasn't. But even there, I felt different. I laughed when I was supposed to. I smiled on cue. But I wasn't there. I was watching my own life from somewhere far away. The worst part wasn't the nights; it was the mornings after, sitting at breakfast while he poured cereal and smiled at my mother like he hadn't destroyed me. He'd ruffle my brother's hair, pat my sister's back, and glance at me with a look that said, I dare you.

I never did.

Instead, I stopped talking unless I had to. My answers became shorter. My laughter disappeared. I'd sit in the tub and scrub until my skin burned, trying to wash off something that wasn't on the surface. I didn't have the words for what had happened, but my body remembered. It remembered every time he walked into the room. Every smell, every sound, every creak in the floor taught my body a language of fear.

And even at nine years old the following year, I couldn't escape the fire again.

Being violated by a "family friend" left another mark, quiet but searing, on my already fragile body. It was the night I learned to compartmentalize, to fold pain into small corners of my mind just to keep breathing.

I was walking to my mother's friend's house, where she was visiting. He stopped me along the way, smiling in that easy, familiar way that makes children lower their guard. Because he was family, or close enough to be called that, I didn't think twice when he said he wanted to talk. I followed him inside.

That's when it happened.

The air in the room shifted, heavy and strange. I remember the sound of the door closing, the faint hum of a nearby fan, the way my heartbeat was so fast it blurred my hearing. My body froze, too shocked to react, too young to understand. I didn't know this was dangerous. I didn't even know there was a name for what was happening to me. When he was finished, he told me to fix my clothes, to tell no one, to "be a good girl." His words were almost gentle, an added cruelty, because they taught me that silence was the price of survival. I believed him. I walked the rest of the way to my mother's friend's house as if nothing had happened, the world spinning around me like a film running out of focus.

It didn't stop there.

It happened again, and again, until I stopped counting. Sometimes at his home, when he'd call me over from playing outside. Sometimes at mine, when he was asked to watch my siblings and me. Each time, he told me it was our little secret. Each time, I felt myself slipping further away from the little girl I had been.

At nine years old, I was doing things that belonged to grown women, and I didn't understand any of it. My body was growing in ways my mind couldn't follow. I learned how to leave my body before the leaving was complete, a kind of spiritual escape that made me look calm on the outside while everything inside me screamed. I started to believe this must be my purpose, that maybe this was why I existed, to be used, to be quiet, to be nothing.

I remember asking God, "Why am I here? Is this all I'm meant for?"

I waited for an answer, but the silence was its own kind of reply.

It didn't finally stop until he moved away. But even then, it didn't really end. Because when he left, it felt like he took a piece of me with him, a piece I didn't know how to name, but felt missing every time I tried to laugh, to trust, to love. That's the thing about childhood trauma: it doesn't end when the perpetrator disappears. It lives in your body, in the quiet rules you make for yourself, in the way you hold your breath when someone walks too close. It changes how you think about home, about safety, about God. It changes you.

Those memories didn't stay in childhood. It followed me. It shaped how I dressed, how I walked, how I loved. I flinched at a touch. I avoided mirrors. I told myself it didn't matter. But it did. Something had fractured deep inside, and I had no idea how to ask for help. I didn't think I could. I was just a little girl. And in the silence of my bedroom, with the lights off and the world asleep, I carried a secret bigger than my body could hold.

That fracture became my depression. It was the shadow that sat beside me for years. It was the reason I cut myself, because I wanted a pain I could control. It was why I prayed for death, because I wanted rest. And when I didn't die, I thought maybe God forgot about me. I started writing then, letters, poems, diary entries, small attempts to stay alive.

May 21, 2001

Dear Diary,

There's a bitterness that lives deep inside, and I don't know when or how it will surface. Sometimes I think about killing myself because of the pain I have in my life. I don't know how to handle it anymore. I'm so tired of crying all the time. People just don't understand the things I've been through. I've tried to kill myself so many times and never succeeded.

That girl, me, was crying out to be seen. What saved her wasn't just faith. It was an expression. I wrote when I couldn't speak. I prayed when I couldn't write. And slowly, I found a version of God who could handle my pain without asking me to hide it. I didn't have to perform. I didn't have to be strong. I could cry and still be held. God became my safe place when there were dark nights.

Even now, I still find myself asking:

Why did I have to endure so much, so soon?

Why didn't anyone notice?

Would I have spoken if someone had just asked, "Are you okay?"

This chapter isn't about answers. It's about truth. And the truth is that depression doesn't always look like sadness. Sometimes it looks like silence. Sometimes it looks like an achievement. Sometimes it looks like being "the strong one." Sometimes it looks like the girl who's always okay, until she's not.

There are so many of us, especially Black girls, smiling through trauma, performing through pain, hiding in plain sight. Until we start talking about mental health as survival, not a shame, we will keep losing people to silence. I lived through *The Blues*. I still live with their echoes. But now I know I'm not the only one. And neither are you.

The Silence I Had To Learn

Silence was the first language I learned. It wasn't taught in words but in glances, the pause in my mother's face when something painful hovered near the surface, the quiet way adults changed the subject when truth got too close. In my family, silence was mistaken for grace, a sign that you could endure without complaint. We didn't name what hurt; we buried it beneath scripture, chores, and phrases like, "what happens in this house stays in this house." I learned early that survival depended on not saying too much, not asking too many questions, and not making anyone uncomfortable. Silence was how I stayed safe. But silence, even when well-intentioned, becomes its own kind of wound. It keeps you small. It convinces you that the truth is dangerous, that your pain is shameful, and that if you ever spoke it, you'd lose the love you were trying to protect.

That silence began in childhood when I was violated by people who should have kept me safe. What happened to me at eight and nine years old was more than a single event; it was the beginning of a fracture that would shape how I saw myself and how I moved through the world. I didn't have the language for sexual abuse. I only knew the heaviness that sat in my chest, the confusion that wrapped around me, and the fear that followed me into every dark room. I told no one because I believed that speaking it aloud would make it worse, that maybe it was somehow my fault. That's what silence does: it shifts the blame inward. It tells you that to keep peace, you must protect the people who hurt you. That's a lie too many children learn before they even understand what love is.

But childhood trauma never stays confined to childhood. It grows up with you. It becomes the lens through which you interpret everything: affection, safety, self-worth, even God. When you've been hurt by someone you trusted, love becomes confusing terrain. Your body doesn't forget what your mind tries to bury. It stays on alert, scanning for danger even in calm moments. For years, I thought that tension was normal, that the pit in my stomach meant I cared deeply, that anxiety meant passion. I confused chaos for chemistry and control for care. It took me years to understand that what I was chasing wasn't love; it was familiarity. My nervous system had been trained to mistake instability for safety.

That is the legacy of unspoken trauma. It doesn't always show up as flashbacks or nightmares. Sometimes it looks like staying busy so you don't have to feel, like attaching to people who replicate your earliest wounds, or like shutting down when someone tries to love you healthily. For a long time, I called that strength. I could hold it all together, excel, make people laugh, and show up for others while quietly collapsing inside. That was my superpower, or so I thought. But survival isn't the same as strength. Survival gets you through; strength helps you rebuild. What I called resilience was really exhaustion. What I called independence was fear of relying on anyone. I didn't know that healing required something I'd spent my whole life avoiding: *vulnerability*.

The silence that once protected me began to suffocate me. It showed up in my depression, the numbness that shadowed even my happiest moments. It showed up in my relationships, where I stayed longer than I should have, mistaking loyalty for love. It showed up in my body, in the tension that never seemed to leave my shoulders. For years, I believed that if I just prayed harder, worked harder, or loved better, I could undo what happened. But trauma doesn't respond to performance. It responds to truth. The first time I named it, called it sexual abuse, violation, trauma, I trembled. But that trembling was freedom. Naming what happened didn't destroy me. It restored me to myself. Because what we don't name owns us.

Healing wasn't a single breakthrough. It was years of therapy, journaling, crying through sessions where words finally found their way out. It was learning that depression wasn't a weakness but a natural response to long-term pain. It was understanding that my body had been protecting me all along, even when I hated how numb I felt. It was unlearning the idea that I had to fix everyone else to be worthy of love. It was the moment I realized that I could release the story that said I was chosen for pain. I wasn't. None of us are. We're just children who were forced to make sense of something senseless, and those interpretations, those coping mechanisms, follow us until we consciously rewrite them.

Faith played a complicated role in my healing. There were seasons when I questioned everything I'd been taught about God. I couldn't reconcile how a loving Creator could watch and stay silent while I suffered. But I also found that faith, when stripped of fear and shame, offered a kind of honesty I hadn't found anywhere else. I stopped performing prayers and started talking to God the way a child speaks to someone who finally listens. I raged, I wept, I doubted, and somehow, I was still held. Healing didn't restore a blind faith; it gave me a wiser one. I learned that faith doesn't erase trauma. It helps you find meaning in survival.

The deeper work of healing came when I learned to listen to my body again. Trauma teaches you to disconnect to live from the neck up and avoid what's happening below. But the body always remembers. The racing heart, the tightening throat, the sudden exhaustion, those were not weaknesses. They were messages. My body was saying, "It wasn't your fault," long before I could believe it. Therapy helped me learn how to respond to those signals with compassion instead of judgment. I stopped asking, "What's wrong with me?" and started asking, "What happened to me, and what do I need now?" That shift changed everything. It made room for peace, real peace, not the silence of suppression, but the calm that comes from safety.

And I want to tell you this, especially if you've carried a secret of your own: silence might have kept you safe once, but you don't need it anymore. You deserve a life that doesn't require hiding. You deserve relationships that don't demand your silence as proof of love. You deserve rest that isn't haunted by memory. Healing doesn't mean the past disappears; it means it no longer decides your future. You may still have moments when the ache returns, but now you'll have the tools to meet it with understanding instead of shame.

Breaking the habit of silence is terrifying because it asks you to believe in your own voice after years of believing it would cost you everything. But the truth is, your voice is the one thing that can't be taken from you; it can only be reclaimed. So, start where you are. Speak your truth, even if it's just a whisper in the beginning. Write it down. Tell it to someone safe. Let your story breathe outside of your body. Healing begins in those small acts of courage, and over time, those acts build a new kind of strength, the kind rooted in honesty, not endurance.

You are not what they did. You are what you survived and who you are becoming. You are living proof that silence can be unlearned, that trauma can be spoken, and that peace, real, lasting peace, is possible.

Therapist's Work For The Reader: Returning To The Root

This exercise is designed to help you begin separating who you were from what happened to you and gently reconnect with the parts of you that learned to survive through silence, sadness, or shutdown. It is best done slowly, in a quiet space, with time to reflect afterward.

Step 1: Locate the Root

Ask yourself: **When did I first feel something shift in me?**

Not just sadness, but a shrinking. A dulling of joy. A moment when you realized you didn't feel safe or seen. You may not remember a specific incident. That's okay. Focus on a general memory or season, age 7, 10, 15… and write freely about:

- What was happening in your environment at the time?
- What beliefs did you start to form about yourself?
- How did you try to protect yourself?

Therapist Insight:

This helps name how early trauma seeds itself as an internal narrative. You weren't "born broken." Something happened. This is the start of separating your identity from your injury.

Step 2: Name the Adaptation

Now ask: **What did I do to survive emotionally during that time?**

This could include:

- Becoming hyper-independent.
- Detaching from your emotions.
- Pleasing others to stay safe.
- Minimizing your needs.
- Using humor, silence, perfectionism, or control.

Write about how these patterns helped you survive back then. Be honest. Be compassionate.

Now ask: **Where are those patterns still active in my adult life, and where are they no longer serving me?**

Therapist Insight:

This is how unresolved trauma quietly continues. Our survival adaptations don't know when the danger is gone. Bringing awareness to them helps the nervous system update its script.

Step 3: Meet the Younger You

CHAPTER 4: THE BLUES

If you feel emotionally ready, write a letter or dialogue from your adult self to your younger self. Keep it honest, clear, and firm, but also deeply gentle.

Include:

- What they didn't deserve to carry
- What you now know about their sadness, shame, or silence
- What you are reclaiming for them now

Now this can be optional: Sit with a childhood photo of yourself while doing this.

Therapist Insight:

This is inner child integration. You're not dismissing the past, you're restoring the self that had to fragment to survive it.

Step 4: Embodiment Check-In

Afterward, ask yourself: **Where do I feel this in my body? What needs soothing? How can I respond to myself in a way that isn't abandoning?**

This may look like:

- Placing a hand on your chest or stomach
- Wrapping yourself in a blanket
- Taking a warm bath or walking barefoot in the grass
- Drinking something warm while breathing deeply

Therapist Insight:

Trauma isn't just emotional, it's somatic. You're teaching your body what safety feels like again. Even small acts of physical self-care send the message: You matter now. I've got you.

Step 5: Set a Ritual of Remembrance

Healing is not an event. It's a rhythm. Choose one weekly ritual that honors your healing. It might be:

- A walk where you speak kind words to yourself
- Lighting a candle and saying, "I'm safe now."
- Writing one truth you no longer believe about yourself, and burning it
- Playing a song that soothes the inner child

Keep it simple. Keep it sacred.

Final Note:

You don't have to heal all at once. You just have to start by seeing yourself clearly, not as broken, but as someone who was deeply impacted and is now deeply worthy of care. You are not behind. You are not too late. You are returning.

Chapter 5

Sixteen and Pregnant

"Sometimes the thing that was never supposed to happen becomes the very thing that saves you."

There are moments in life that divide everything into before and after. Before sixteen, I was a teenager who still believed I could outsmart the pain that ran through my family like blood. I wanted more for myself than what I had seen. I studied hard, joined cheerleading, and nurtured quiet dreams about attending college and building a life that was stable, meaningful, and my own. Even though I was growing up in chaos, fatherlessness, abuse, and instability, I carried a quiet conviction that I would not become another statistic. I had survived too much to end up stuck in the same cycle. I told myself I was going to be the one who made it out. And then, at sixteen, I found myself staring at a pregnancy test that said otherwise. That's all it took for my world to tilt.

The day I took the test, everything around me felt heavy with knowing, even before I saw the result. I had been sick for days, tired, nauseous, uneasy in my own body, but I told myself it was nothing. When I finally bought the test, I felt the weight of every eye in the store following me as if my shame were visible. I remember the cashier's half-smile, the soft judgment in her silence. I went home, locked the bathroom door, and sat on the edge of the bathtub, holding the box like a secret. I read the instructions twice and whispered a prayer I didn't know how to finish. When the two lines appeared, I didn't scream or cry. I froze. Time stopped moving, and I just stared at it. I remember thinking, "This can't be happening. Not to me."

That night, I didn't sleep. I lay in bed staring at the ceiling, replaying every decision, every moment that led me here. I kept asking myself how I could have been so careful and still ended up pregnant. I felt a mixture of disbelief, fear, and self-blame. Somewhere deep down, that old narrative, you always ruin everything, began to whisper again. The shame was immediate and total. It felt like I had confirmed what the world already expected of girls like me: young, Black, and from a broken home.

I tried to carry the secret for a while. I went to school, smiled at my friends, went to cheer tryouts, and pretended nothing had changed. I didn't have room for disruption when I was finally doing something for myself. But everything had. My body was betraying me one symptom at a time. When my appetite disappeared, I brushed it off as nerves, or maybe bad cafeteria food, as I had once before. Later, sitting in Popeyes with friends, I pushed food around on my plate as the nausea reached the surface. When I began to vomit, one friend joked, "Girl, you pregnant?" We all laughed it off, too quickly, too loudly. But inside, I knew they were right.

CHAPTER 5: SIXTEEN AND PREGNANT

When I finally told the baby's father, his face went blank. He didn't yell or panic; he just said, "We'll figure it out." But we didn't. He told my mother before I could. I will never forget the look on her face when she found out. It wasn't anger. It wasn't disappointment. It was something deeper, like a quiet recognition that history had repeated itself in front of her eyes. I braced for punishment, but she didn't yell. She just sat in silence, then exhaled and said softly, "We'll get through this." That stillness was both comforting and heartbreaking because I knew what she meant. She had gotten through her own storms, and now she was preparing to help me do the same.

Telling my grandparents was harder. My grandfather's intuition told him before my words did. He didn't ask; he simply said, "You're going to be okay," in that tone elders use when they've already decided to hold you up. My grandmother was the last to know. I expected rejection, but instead, she wrapped me in her arms, touched my belly, and said, "This is still a blessing." Her grace didn't erase my fear, but it softened the edges of my shame.

Pregnancy at sixteen isn't something you can prepare for. It changes not only your body but your entire sense of self. One moment you're thinking about prom, and the next you're calculating how to afford diapers. I felt like my life had been split in two: the person I was before the test and the one I was now forced to become. I wasn't ready to be a mother, but I didn't have the privilege of choosing readiness. The months that followed were a blur of exhaustion, fear, and quiet determination.

I remember walking through the hallways of school with my belly just beginning to show, the whispers trailing behind me like smoke. Teachers looked at me with pity. Classmates with curiosity. Adults with judgment. No one asked how I was doing; they only asked, "What are you going to do now?", as if motherhood at sixteen were a life sentence instead of a life shift. There were days I felt invisible and others when I felt too visible. Either way, I felt alone.

Still, something inside me refused to collapse completely. I began to see this baby, not as punishment but as purpose. In the Spring semester of 2003, she arrived, small and perfect, with a cry that filled the quiet spaces of my life. I remember the weight of her against my chest, the warmth of her skin, and the strange realization that I was responsible for another human being. It was overwhelming. It was beautiful. And it was terrifying.

Motherhood does not wait for your healing to be complete. It doesn't care if you're still a child yourself. It doesn't pause to make sure you've processed your trauma or built your identity. It just hands you this new life and expects you to become what you never had, a safe place. I wanted to be that for her. But some days, I could barely be that for myself. There were mornings I woke up determined to change the world, and nights I cried quietly in the dark, wondering if I'd already failed her.

A few years after my high school graduation, I found myself living the very life I had promised I'd never repeat. The father of my child began drifting in and out of jail, and I carried resentment like a second skin. I worked multiple jobs, juggled classes in trade school, and counted every dollar twice. I was trying to build a home, a future, and a new identity all at once. But there were times the struggle nearly consumed me. There were days when the refrigerator was empty, the lights threatened to go off, and I felt the pull of desperation.

I remember one night vividly. I was sitting on the edge of my bed, bills spread out around me, my daughter asleep in the next room. I was exhausted, mentally, emotionally, spiritually. A friend of my friend had offered me money before, making his intentions clear. I had always ignored him. But that night, when I counted the cash in my wallet and came up short, his number came to mind. It wasn't desire that drove me to consider it; it was survival. I held my phone in my hand, staring at his name, my stomach in knots. I thought about what $300 could fix: groceries, overdue bills, and I also thought about what it would cost me. The weight of my daughter's future and my dignity sat on opposite sides of a scale. For the first time, I realized how easily desperation could push a woman toward a choice she swore she'd never make. I cried until my throat hurt. Then I prayed, not for money, but for strength. I asked God to help me hold on to myself. I prayed, "God, I don't want this. I don't want to sell myself. I don't want to become someone I can't look in the mirror. Please, make a way." He must have heard my prayers because the next thing I knew, I finally texted him back, all I wrote was, "I don't need your help anymore." I turned off my phone, took a deep breath, and felt something shift inside me. It was small, but it was sacred. That single act of refusal was the first time I truly chose myself. It was the first time I stood in the gap between who I was and who I wanted to become.

Pregnancy at sixteen didn't destroy my life. It dismantled the illusions I had about control, worthiness, and strength. It forced me to rebuild from the ground up, without a blueprint and without certainty. It taught me that resilience isn't built in calm seasons; it's born in survival. My daughter didn't just give me a reason to live; she gave me a reason to live differently.

When I look back now, I don't see a ruined girl. I see a young woman who was scared, unprepared, and still brave enough to keep going. I see someone who didn't yet understand that her story wasn't an ending but an origin story. Becoming a mother didn't erase my pain. It revealed my purpose.

This Is Not The End Of You

Teen pregnancy is one of the most misunderstood experiences a young woman can go through. The moment those two pink lines appear, society doesn't just react; it judges. Labels arrive before compassion. You are no longer a girl with dreams; you are a cautionary tale. Every look, every whisper, every statistic says the same thing: you've ruined your life. But those narratives are built by people who have never had to make grown decisions with a child's heart, or who have never felt what it's like to be responsible for a life while still trying to build their own.

No young girl dreams of becoming a mother at sixteen. It's not something written on vision boards or spoken aloud during career day. Teen pregnancy doesn't begin with sex; it begins with silence. It begins with unmet needs, unspoken pain, and a search for love in places that promise belonging but deliver consequences. It begins when emotional neglect feels normal, when affection is confused with attention, when no one teaches you that your worth exists outside of being chosen. For many of us, pregnancy wasn't the first time our boundaries were crossed; it was the first time the world noticed.

In communities like ours, the conversation about teen pregnancy often stops at shame. We're told what we did wrong, but not what went wrong around us. No one asks about the environment that shaped the decision, or the absence of conversations that could have prevented it. No one talks about the fatherlessness, the cycles of trauma, or the hunger to feel wanted that so many girls carry long before they ever carry a child. Instead, we're met with silence, and that silence becomes its own kind of inheritance.

When I think about that sixteen-year-old version of myself, I see a young woman standing at the intersection of survival and identity. I wasn't trying to ruin my life; I was trying to feel loved. But love that grows out of unhealed wounds will always cost you more than it gives. That's what we rarely talk about: how early trauma sets the stage for choices made from emptiness. When you've been conditioned to mistake chaos for connection, you don't notice the red flags; you mistake them for attention. And by the time you realize you're repeating the same story, the results are already alive and breathing in your arms.

But here's the truth: motherhood does not erase your potential. It reshapes it. It demands that you grow in directions you never thought you could. It pushes you to hold two things at once: grief and gratitude, regret and resilience. You can love your child deeply and still mourn the life you lost. You can be a devoted mother and still be figuring out how to mother yourself. You can carry diapers in one hand and a degree in the other. The world may not permit you to hold those contradictions, but they are real, and they are yours.

To the girl who found out she was pregnant and thought her life was over: I know what it feels like to cry quietly in your room, wondering how you'll tell your family, how you'll finish school, how you'll face your friends. I know what it feels like to carry both shame and hope, to want to disappear and still want to be seen. You may think this is the end of your story, but it's not. It's the beginning of a different one, one that will require courage, but will also reveal your strength in ways you never imagined.

There will be hard days. Days when the bills outnumber your dollars. Days when exhaustion feels like another child you have to carry. Days when you question if you're enough. You will wonder if you made a mistake too big to recover from. But those days are not the measure of your worth. They are proof that you are still standing, still trying, still showing up. Survival is not failure. It is evidence that you are alive, still capable of rewriting the narrative that was written for you.

To the educators, counselors, clinicians, and family members reading this: teen mothers don't need your judgment; they need your understanding. You cannot shame a girl into healing. You cannot scold her into stability. What you can do is listen. Ask her what she believes about herself. Ask her what she's afraid of. Ask her who taught her that love must hurt or that her worth is negotiable. Those questions do more than offer empathy; they invite her to rewrite her story. And then listen, not to respond, but to understand. You might find that her story doesn't just explain her pregnancy, it explains her pain.

We need to stop treating teen pregnancy as a moral failure and start treating it as an indicator of where our systems have failed. It is not just a personal decision; it's a public reflection of the ways we neglect our girls emotionally, spiritually, and mentally. If we want to change the outcomes, we must begin earlier. We must talk about self-worth and boundaries long before sex becomes a conversation. We must create safe spaces where girls can speak without fear, where they are believed when they say they're hurting, and where their bodies are not their only currency for love.

I want every young woman who has ever carried shame in her womb or guilt in her heart to know this: you are not disqualified from joy. You are not behind. You are not broken beyond repair. Your story is not defined by how it began, but by how you choose to continue it. Motherhood may have interrupted your plans, but it didn't end your purpose. There will come a time, maybe years later, when you will look back and see that this was the moment you began to rise. The girl who thought her life was over will become the woman who built a new one from the ashes. She will learn to trust herself again, to dream again, to love without losing herself again.

To every woman who ever carried a child while still a child herself, I see you. You are not ruined. You are rewritten. Your baby is not your punishment; they are your reminder that even in the midst of brokenness, life still insists on blooming.

This chapter in your life is not a full stop or a period. It's a semicolon. You're allowed to continue the sentence.

You're allowed to pivot. You're allowed to revise the story and write new paragraphs filled with purpose, peace, and power. And when someone asks, "What changed you?" You can say, "Motherhood didn't end me. It refined me." Your story is still unfolding. When you look back, this won't just be the moment everything changed; it'll be the moment you decide to rise anyway. Because what the world called a mistake was actually the beginning of your becoming.

Therapist's Work For The Reader: Rewriting The Narrative

This exercise is about reclamation, not of your past, but of your voice. Many of us grew up in environments where our mistakes became our identity, where shame shaped our silence, and where we learned to equate worth with perfection. But you are not the sum of your past decisions. You are the author of what comes next.

These steps are meant to guide you, gently, honestly, and with compassion, through the process of transforming your story from survival into strength.

Step 1: Name the Narrative

Write down the first word or phrase that comes to mind when you think about your story as a teen, the word that still carries weight. It might be a mistake, embarrassment, or failure.

Then, ask yourself: **Who gave me that word?** Was it a parent, a teacher, a church, a rumor, or your own inner critic?

Now, write a new word beside it, one that feels redemptive, even if it's only aspirational right now. Words like resilient, becoming, brave, or evolving.

This is not about denying the past; it's about choosing a new language for who you are becoming. Language is power. What you name yourself shapes how you move forward.

Step 2: Reclaim the Body

For many women, especially those who have experienced early pregnancy, assault, or shame, the body becomes a battleground. We learn to see it as something to control, cover, or correct. But your body has always been your witness, not your enemy.

- Find a mirror.
- Take one long look at yourself, not the edited version, not the posed one, but you.
- Then, place your hand on your stomach, the same place that once held fear or life or both, and say aloud:

"This body has carried me. This body remembers, but it also heals. I am learning to live in it without shame."

Repeat it until the words begin to sound like the truth. Healing begins when the body is invited back into the story.

Step 3: Confront the Inherited Beliefs

Reflect on what you were taught about womanhood, motherhood, and worth. Ask yourself:

- What messages about my body, sexuality, or mistakes did I inherit?
- Who told me that love had to be earned through pain?

CHAPTER 5: SIXTEEN AND PREGNANT

- Where did I learn that redemption wasn't possible for me?

Now, counter each of those beliefs with truth statements that affirm your agency. For example:

- "I am not dirty; I am human."
- "I can be both a mother and a dreamer."
- "I am not my circumstances; I am my choices going forward."

This step may bring up emotion, and that's okay. Unlearning is emotional work. You are not rejecting your past; you are reframing it.

Step 4: Create a New Vision

Close your eyes and imagine yourself ten years from now, not the fantasy version, but the real, healed you.

- What does she look like?
- How does she carry herself?
- Who is in her life?
- What kind of love surrounds her?

Now, write her a letter from your current self. Tell her what you're learning. Tell her what you're afraid of. Tell her what you hope to become.

Then, sign it with something powerful, with faith, with courage, with becoming. Keep that letter. It's a contract between who you are and who you are still becoming.

Step 5: Set a Symbol of Continuation

Find something small, a bracelet, a candle, a stone, a piece of paper folded in your wallet, that reminds you of continuation. Not perfection. Not closure. Continuation.

Every time you touch it, let it remind you that you are still in motion, still worthy of joy, still rewriting the story. Because what once felt like the end was actually a beginning.

Therapist Insight: The Power of Narrative Repair

In trauma therapy, we often talk about narrative repair, the process of reworking the meaning of your story so that it no longer controls you. This isn't about denial or erasure. It's about perspective. When you begin to see your younger self with compassion instead of criticism, the shame that once silenced you begins to dissolve. You stop defining yourself by what happened and start defining yourself by how you choose to heal.

Your story deserves to be told, not as a tragedy but as a testimony. When you are ready to tell it, you won't need validation. You'll already know that the woman who survived it is the same woman who rebuilt it.

Chapter 6

Repeat Offender

"It is funny how after a bad relationship, it can propel you in a new direction that God has destined for you."

Some women break the cycle at the first red flag, and some women don't even know they're in a cycle yet. I was the second kind. I didn't wake up one day and say, "Let me keep choosing men who can't love me." What happened was slower and sadder than that. Somewhere between wanting to be loved and needing to be chosen, I became the woman who went back, back to familiar pain, back to lopsided love, back to what looked like attention but felt like emptiness. I saw the red flags. I heard the caution from friends. I even felt my own body tighten in warning. But when you grow up emotionally hungry, even dysfunction looks nourishing. When you're starving, even crumbs start to look like a feast.

For a long time, I thought it was just bad luck, wrong time, wrong city, wrong men. But eventually I had to tell the truth: I was searching for my father in men who were still searching for themselves. I was dating a wound. So every time something ended, I didn't stop to breathe or heal or ask, "What in me made this feel like love?" I just moved on. New face, same ache. That's why I call this chapter Repeat Offender. Not because they were all terrible men, though some of them did real harm, but because I kept committing the same emotional crime against myself: abandoning myself to be chosen by them. And this is my rap sheet.

Relationships 1 and 2

Before 2004, I'd already had a few little flings, teenage, short-lived, cute-but-empty situationships. Nothing serious, nothing stable. But even in those early ones, a pattern was forming: I was always the one pouring more. I mistook intensity for intimacy, attention for affection, and consistency for commitment.

I met the first real one online, back when it felt harmless and fun, before social media became what it is now. He was funny, attentive, and actually listened. That was rare for me. I was a young mom, carrying more responsibility than most girls my age, and he wasn't scared off by that. He asked about my daughter. He made room for both of us in conversation. That alone made him stand out. We talked for months, then lost touch, life doing what life does. I found his picture later while cleaning, and something in me sparked, like, *oh yeah, him*. I reached out again, and this time the connection deepened fast. The affection was real, or at least it felt real. When I thought I might be pregnant, he didn't panic; he celebrated. He opened a bank account for a baby we didn't even know existed yet. That's not something many men do, especially not at that age. In that moment, I thought, *this could be it.*

Then he moved out of state to take care of his family. That's when the distance started to expose the holes. I told myself I could do long distance. But when you've been abandoned before, emotional distance feels like abandonment all over again. So I did what unhealed people do: I tried to fill the gap. I started seeing someone local. He wasn't better. He was just there. I told myself it was "just talking," but the truth is, I didn't know how to be without male attention. I was trying to hold onto the man I loved and the man who was nearby at the same time.

Then I made another mistake, I told a "friend." Not just the surface parts. The whole thing. I trusted "girl code" to cover what my maturity should've handled. So when I began making plans to visit the long-distance guy and bring that same friend along, because he asked me to bring a friend, she later told the man back home everything. Every. Single. Detail. He confronted me at work with facts only she could have given him. I had to call the other man right in front of him. It was humiliating, and I remember crying not just because I'd been caught, but because I'd lost the one man who had shown me something secure.

When I confronted my friend, she said, "Well, he was my friend first." And that's when it clicked: I had handed sacred information to someone who didn't know how to hold it. I cut her off. I didn't have the tools to say, "I was betrayed too," but I knew enough to say, "I won't give you this access to me again."

Both relationships ended. One because of geography, one because of truth. And even then, I didn't stop to ask why I needed two men at once. I just told myself, "Well, that didn't work," and kept going. But the lesson was already in the room: when you don't believe you're worthy of steady love, you will create chaos to explain the instability you're used to. Until I learned to sit in my own silence and face the girl underneath the pain, I kept repeating the same cycle.

Relationship 3

By the time the next man came along, I had my own place. My daughter and I were finding rhythm. From the outside, it looked like stability. But stability without healing is just quiet, and quiet can make unprocessed pain sound louder.

He came in slowly. Nothing flashy, nothing grand. Just present. And because presence was something I'd craved for so long, I mistook accessibility for compatibility. I let him stay over. Then stay more. Then stay regularly. I told myself we were "building." What I was actually doing was giving full access to someone who hadn't proven he could steward it.

The first few months were calm. Too calm. Looking back, I should've known the silence wasn't peace, it was the calm before a storm I didn't know I'd invited into my home. Then came the night that changed it. It was after 2 a.m. I woke up and noticed his phone was lit on the nightstand. It was as if the glow pulled me out of my sleep like a siren. I leaned over and saw a name I didn't know. I got out of bed, picked up the phone, and walked to the other room like a woman on a mission. I called the number. She answered on the second ring and in that tired, unbothered voice women use when they don't know they're talking to "the girlfriend," she told me everything as if she had been waiting for a stage. She told me how they met and how he claimed to be single. How he took her out, met her family, and brought her flowers. Flowers I had never seen. That stung more than the cheating, knowing someone else got the softness I was begging for.

I snapped. I put my daughter safely with my roommate, and I went off. I threw his things out. I yelled. I tried to break his things. It was anger, yes, but it was more than that; it was grief for the version of me who kept trying to earn basic respect. That explosion cost me more than a man. It cost me a friendship with my roommate. She saw a side of me that wasn't polished, wasn't composed, and after that, we were never the same. And still, I let him back.

That's the part people don't get about trauma bonds. You can know and still return. I knew he lied. I knew he entertained other women. I knew trust was gone. But I stayed because the pain of being alone felt, in that season, worse than the pain of being disrespected. That is what unhealed attachment does: it tells you something is better than nothing, even if that something is slowly eroding you.

After it ended for good, I didn't turn inward. I spiraled. I slept with multiple men in a short period because I wanted to feel wanted, and sex is the fastest counterfeit for belonging. I drank, smoked, numbed. I was functioning, going to work, being a mom, but emotionally, I was in free fall.

That relationship taught me this: letting a man into your home is not the same as letting him into your life. And proximity is not the same as partnership.

Relationship 4

I told myself I was going to take a break. We all say that. "I'm done with men." "It's just me, God, and me." "I'm focusing on my child." And sometimes we mean it, but often what we really mean is, "I need love to work this time." So when the next one came, I convinced myself he was different. He wasn't even my type. He was loud, confident, and cocky. He moved fast, and fast felt flattering. Within a week, I was at Thanksgiving with his family. Within a month, I had a key. He bought me a necklace. He made space for me in his world. And for someone with an old rejection wound, being given access felt like being chosen. But speed is not the same as sincerity.

I started to see things. Facebook messages. People in his circle have opinions about me. A cousin who was a little too interested. A former friend who introduced us, whose family suddenly had thoughts about my place in his life. I brought it up calmly, and he blew up. Not because I was wrong, but because I looked. That's how control works: it calls curiosity "disrespect."

Then I found out he was still in love with someone else. Actively. Not ex-love, not old love, current love. I was the placeholder. I was the comfort. I was the woman who was "good to him," but not the woman he wanted to claim as his own. That is a unique kind of humiliation, when you realize you are doing main-character labor in a role someone else already holds in his heart. I snapped again. Drove to his apartment. Ripped things up. Cried. Raged. His sisters retaliated with lies. They called my phone. They brought my job into it. All of that fallout, and we hadn't even been together a year.

That six-month relationship cost me friends, income, peace, and dignity. But it also gave me language: this isn't just "men are trash." This is me returning to chaos because chaos is what I know.

Relationship 5

They say rock bottom has a basement, but I wasn't prepared for how deep I could sink. After the chaos, the lies, the job loss, the public unraveling, you'd think I would've chosen peace, solitude, or stillness. But when you've spent years confusing attachment with love, quietness can feel like abandonment. Instead of turning inward to do the work, I did what I'd always done: I reached for someone.

I met him on my birthday. I was still tender from the previous breakup, still embarrassed, still mad at myself. I should've been healing. Instead, I picked up another distraction. He was rough around the edges, mysterious, the kind of man who felt a little dangerous. And because part of me was still addicted to chaos, I leaned toward him. It wasn't a relationship. It was sex, convenience, and fantasy. We never dated publicly. We weren't building anything. We weren't talking about the future. I was just available. And because I was available, he treated me like I was. I told myself I was in control, that I wouldn't get too deep this time, but control is an illusion when you're emotionally starving.

There were signs. So many signs. When I found the condom in his trash that wasn't from me, I saw it. I saw exactly what this was. And I still stayed. Not because I didn't know better, but because I didn't yet believe I deserved better. I stayed for two years in something that had no name because I was still convinced I could be the exception. He told me he didn't want a relationship, and I heard, "You just haven't met the right woman," so I auditioned like I was her. This is why I tell women now: if he says he doesn't want more, believe him. You are not the loophole.

Then came the night I couldn't deny it. I was out downtown with friends, laughing, finally trying to enjoy myself. I saw him across the street. Before I could get to him, another woman walked right up, hugged him like she'd done it before, and they started talking like they weren't strangers at all. I walked up just as they were exchanging numbers. He barely flinched. "She's just someone from high school," he said. "It's not even like that." I believed him. Not because it made sense, but because I wasn't ready to face the truth. I wasn't ready to admit I had given two years of access to someone who hadn't even tried to claim me. But that's what we do when we're starving. We believe the smallest version of the story, even if it means we don't have to walk away.

So we kept going. Kept sleeping together. Kept pretending. But something started shifting in me. My body felt it before my mouth could say it. I started to feel resentment rise, not loud, just steady. I didn't want him to touch me anymore, but I let him anyway because I'd convinced myself that being the one he saw physically, even if I wasn't the one he saw emotionally, was still better than nothing. But it wasn't. It was a slow erosion of my soul. That slow disgust is important because that's usually where women finally turn. Not at the cheating, not at the lies, but at the moment our own spirit says, "I don't want to participate in this anymore."

Around that time, I also started to want more from life. Not even a ring or a wedding, just respect, reciprocity, and intention. I started answering more slowly. Going out less. Letting his texts sit. My energy was shifting, and he could feel it. That's when he finally came to my house. After two years of always going to him, he walked through my front door like a visitor in a place he never truly wanted to belong to. That alone told me everything. We were intimate that night, but I wasn't fully there. My heart had already started moving on. By then, I'd met someone kind, not perfect, but attentive, and that contrast showed me what I'd been tolerating.

July was the last month I saw him. There was no big fight, no dramatic closure, no speech. It just ended, quietly, almost politely. But in that silence was a small rebirth. I was finally beginning to understand: love should not feel like desperation. Attention is not affection. Waiting for someone to become what you need is its own form of heartbreak.

That situationship taught me the cost of choosing potential over reality. It taught me how loneliness can talk you into accepting half-love and unreturned calls. It taught me that sex without intimacy is not empowerment, it's emptiness with a nice outfit on. But most of all, it taught me this: you cannot make someone want to choose you, and every time you try, you lose a little more of yourself in the attempt.

Relationship 6

CHAPTER 6: REPEAT OFFENDER

They say when the student is ready, the teacher appears. But sometimes, the "teacher" doesn't show up in a classroom; he shows up wearing charm, intensity, and red flags disguised as romance. He becomes the test you didn't study for but needed to pass to finally graduate from your own patterns. That's what this relationship was for me, not just another heartbreak, but a reckoning. It wasn't just about him; it was about every unhealed version of me that kept believing I had to earn love.

He wasn't my type at first glance. He carried himself with that kind of confidence that borders on arrogance, sharp edges, commanding presence, the kind of man who walks into a room as if it belongs to him. Part of me found it irritating. Another part found it magnetic. I should've listened to that inner nudge that whispered, "Be careful with this one." But I was tired of being careful. Tired of feeling like I was always auditioning for love and losing the part. So when he came around, I jumped in, fast, unguarded, and desperate to believe maybe this time, it would be different.

In the beginning, it was intoxicating. He called me "baby girl," brushed my back when we walked through crowds, and made me feel seen in the subtle ways that feel personal to a woman who's been overlooked for too long. He wasn't gentle, but he was present, and I mistook intensity for intimacy. I wanted to believe that this time would be different. But the truth was, I was the same me. Still looking for love to validate what I hadn't yet healed in myself. And the more he drew me in, the more I lost myself. What I didn't realize then was that this wasn't a love story; it was a power exchange.

The rules began subtly. Small comments about what I wore. Who did I talk to? How long did it take me to respond to a text? Then they grew. He needed to know where I was, what I was doing, and who I was with. If I didn't answer quickly enough, accusations flew: *You're lying. You don't respect me. You're hiding something.* The control crept in quietly until it became normal. Meanwhile, I still hadn't met his mother. Or his family. "She doesn't want to meet another one of my girlfriends unless I'm serious," he'd said once. And I told myself that made sense, that I just needed to wait my turn to be "serious." But deep down, it didn't feel right. Something about the distance between his words and his actions never sat well in my spirit.

Then came the night that split everything open. We were supposed to go to the movies. I was running late, not hours late, just enough for him to notice. He called over and over, each call more aggressive than the last. When I finally answered, I lied and said I was already on the road, trying to avoid another argument. I forgot to mute my phone, and he heard the sound of my car alarm chirping, proof that I was still home.

He exploded.

"You're lying to me now? Over something this simple?"

His voice cut sharply, rising with every sentence.

"You don't give a damn about my time. You're selfish."

"You always do this."

I sat in my car, shaking, trying to make sense of how a small delay had turned into an all-out war. His anger felt disproportionate, but in that moment, I was too used to chaos to call it what it was: emotional manipulation. I drove to his apartment anyway and sat in my car, silent and numb, before going into his apartment. I didn't want to fight, but I also didn't know how to stop the pattern of appeasing men who punished me for being human. That night, something inside me cracked. Not a clean break, just a hairline fracture in my denial. While in the car, I called a close friend, one of the few who hadn't grown tired of my relationship drama. With this friend, I had kept the relationship quiet, partly to protect it, mostly because I was embarrassed. However, that night I needed someone who could remind me what sanity sounded like. I cried as soon as he answered.

"I don't know what I'm doing," I said.

"He's mad because I was late, and now he's flipping out. I told a little lie to keep the peace, but it backfired, and now he's losing it."

His voice softened, but his tone changed.

"Who?" he asked.

I swallowed. "Who what?"

He asked, "Who is the guy you're talking about?"

I hesitated at first. When I said his name, there was a silence so heavy it made my stomach twist.

"Wait... are you serious?" he asked slowly.

"Yeah, why?" My voice was barely above a whisper.

He sighed deeply. "Whit... I hate to be the one to tell you this, but you need to get out. Fast. That dude is no good."

My stomach dropped. "What do you mean? What happened?"

I pressed him for details, but he wouldn't give specifics. "It's not my story to tell," he said. "But I know someone who can tell you hers." He gave me the name and number of a woman, an ex of the guy I was in a relationship with. He said she'd been through it, that she'd talk to me if I called. I hesitated. My pride resisted. But my gut knew I needed to know.

"She'll talk to you," he said.

"Call her. Listen. Don't brush it off."

The next day, I called. My hands were trembling when she answered. She didn't sound surprised. "I was wondering when someone would call me about him again," she said. My stomach dropped. That one sentence told me everything. We introduced ourselves and started comparing stories. The lies. The gaslighting. The way he'd twist everything to make her feel crazy. The emotional push and pull kept her off balance. Every sentence she spoke felt like déjà vu. Then she said something that froze me in place.

"There was always something off with him," she said slowly.

"But what really got to me was his relationship with his mom." She hesitated, like she was weighing how much truth to give me.

"It wasn't normal," she continued.

"There were no boundaries. I came home early from work once, and they were in the bedroom watching something on TV... and it wasn't a family movie. Let's just say that. It felt wrong. Everything in me knew it was wrong. When I questioned it, he made me feel crazy."

I remember gripping the phone, my pulse pounding. She kept talking, her voice shaking now.

"I don't know what they had going on," she said softly.

"After that, I couldn't unsee it. And his mother hated me. Despised me. It was like I threatened something sacred between them. There were things I'll never fully understand, but the energy in that house wasn't right."

Silence sat between us, heavy, knowing, sickening. My mind started reeling. When we finally hung up, I sat on the edge of my bed and stared at the wall. For a long time. No tears came. No screaming. Just stillness. Sometimes truth doesn't bring relief; it brings clarity, and clarity can hurt like hell.

I thought about the times he wouldn't let me come over when she was in town. The uneasiness I'd felt but brushed off. The way he protected that relationship more fiercely than he ever protected ours. It all made sense now, a twisted kind of sense that left me nauseous.

That night, I confronted him. He exploded again, defensive, loud, cruel. "Why would you believe some girl you don't even know over me?" he shouted. "You really think I'd do something like that?" He flipped it, accused me of being gullible, jealous, and insecure. But I didn't argue back. I didn't have to. The silence between us said everything.

After that, nothing was the same. The relationship began to rot from the inside out. The arguments became more frequent. The affection disappeared. The lies became harder to ignore. The cheating more obvious. The manipulation more shameless. And still, I stayed, longer than I should have, longer than made sense. Not because I loved him, but because I didn't want to feel like I had failed again. I didn't want to start over or admit that I'd once again mistaken possession for partnership.

By September, I was emotionally bankrupt. I wasn't sleeping. I wasn't laughing. I was just existing, going through the motions, but spiritually hollow. That's when I wrote *The Last Straw*. Because that relationship wasn't just another heartbreak; it was the mirror I could no longer look away from. It showed me the pattern I'd been repeating, the woman I had become to survive it, and the one I needed to reclaim to heal it.

He didn't just break my heart. He broke the cycle. And for that, as painful as it was, I'm grateful. Because sometimes the person who hurts you the most is also the one who pushes you to finally choose yourself.

Until I Noticed The Pattern Was Me

Some chapters in life don't end quietly; they rupture. And this one, it wasn't just another heartbreak. It was the loud, unflinching mirror I had spent years avoiding. For the first time, I had to stop pointing fingers at the people who hurt me and turn that hard truth inward. I was the common denominator.

That realization was devastating. Because it's easier to believe you've just been unlucky than to face the fact that your pain has a pattern, one that you've been helping to maintain. I didn't title this chapter *Repeat Offender* because of the men I dated, though some of their behavior deserved consequences. I titled it that because I was the one repeating the agonizing sentence. I was the one reentering the same emotional prison, locking the door from the inside, and convincing myself that this time, maybe the walls would feel like home.

That's what unresolved trauma does: it doesn't just haunt your past; it scripts your present. It chooses for you. It colors your judgment. It filters your definition of love through the lens of pain. The brain wires itself around patterns that feel safe, even if they're harmful. Unless we interrupt that programming, we will always seek what once wounded us. Because safety and familiarity are not the same thing, but trauma doesn't know that.

If you learned early that love was inconsistent or conditional, you will chase people who replicate that exact rhythm, not because it feels good, but because it feels normal. And "normal" becomes the baseline you unconsciously measure love by. That's why you can end up mistaking unpredictability for chemistry, or silence for peace, or anxiety for passion. The body confuses the feeling of danger with the feeling of home. And until you learn to tell the difference, you'll keep choosing what feels familiar, even when it hurts.

You can't heal what you refuse to name, and you can't break a pattern you're still romanticizing. For years, I told myself the story that I was loyal, forgiving, hopeful, that all I needed was a man who would see the real me. But beneath those noble words was a deeper truth: I didn't believe I was worthy of calm, only chaos. I thought love was supposed to hurt before it healed. That was the lie I inherited and kept rehearsing.

That defining moment came when I realized I wasn't just unlucky in love. I was unaware in love. I was performing the same role in different relationships: the fixer, the forgiver, the one who made excuses. I had confused endurance with intimacy. I didn't know that love could be safe because I had never seen it modeled that way.

Romanticization is often a trauma response, a subconscious reenactment of early attachment wounds disguised as passion. We mistake unpredictability for excitement because, somewhere in our developmental years, we learned that love was something to be earned, not something freely given. When emotional unavailability or inconsistency was normalized in childhood, the nervous system became wired to associate longing with connection and pain with attachment. That wiring doesn't just vanish; it becomes the compass we unconsciously use in adult relationships. So we find ourselves drawn to the same emotional dynamics, dressed up in new bodies and new names. And when we cling to the fantasy of saving someone or being chosen after enduring mistreatment, we romanticize dysfunction. And what we romanticize, we repeat.

When that last relationship fell apart, I resisted the urge to rush into another one. Instead of trying to reassemble the pieces, I sat in the rubble. I studied it. I asked better questions. Not, "Why did he do this to me?" but "Why did I stay?" Not, "Why do I attract broken people?" but "Why do I feel safest when I'm shrinking to be loved?" Those questions hurt, but they also healed. Because every question brought me closer to the truth. That's the moment I realized: my healing wouldn't come from finding a better partner. It would come from becoming a better partner to myself.

Healing didn't make me invincible; it made me aware. It didn't erase my triggers or rewrite my history. It simply gave me language, the ability to name what I was doing and why I was doing it. That's the first step in unlearning. Awareness doesn't immediately free you, but it gives you the power to choose differently the next time. And that's where change begins, in the pause between your old pattern and your new decision.

Patterns don't break overnight. They unravel slowly, decision by decision. They weaken each time you choose not to answer a call from someone who only knows how to love you halfway. They shift every time you say "no" to what drains you, even when it still feels familiar. Healing means learning to tolerate peace after years of chaos. It's learning that calm doesn't mean boring; it means safe. Eventually, you will have to decide that the cost of repeating the offense is too high. Even if you don't know what "healthy" looks like yet, you have to stop choosing what hurts. Healing doesn't require perfection; it requires honesty. You can't outgrow what you refuse to outface.

I no longer see myself as the woman who failed at love. I see myself as the woman who finally stopped confusing suffering with depth. The one who learned that love that costs your peace is too expensive. The one who realized that sometimes losing someone isn't a punishment, it's protection. So if you're reading this and recognizing yourself in my reflection, know this: your story doesn't end in repetition. The pattern ends when you decide to stop rehearsing it. That's where freedom begins, not when someone else finally chooses you, but when you finally choose yourself.

Chapter 7

Blank Canvas

"Healing begins when you question the beliefs you inherited and give yourself permission to replace them with truth."

After the last relationship, something in me finally cracked, but not in the way it had before. Not like all the other times I tried to bounce back, glued together with denial and determination. This time, I wasn't interested in pretending I was fine. I didn't want to be resilient. I wanted to be new. I was done trying to rebuild the same broken version of myself. I had spent years trying to fix what life had shattered, pouring myself into people, patching old wounds with new relationships, dressing trauma up as strength. But nothing I tried ever worked. Every time I thought I'd found love, I ended up right back in the same emotional ruins.

I was exhausted. Not just emotionally, but spiritually. My soul felt thin, like I'd been scraped down to nothing. I was tired of chasing the idea of being loved, tired of carrying guilt that didn't belong to me, tired of performing as though I had everything under control when control was the very thing that kept me bound. Somewhere between the heartbreaks, the betrayals, and the constant striving, I realized: my way wasn't working.

For the first time, I stopped trying to fix myself. I stopped chasing. I stopped running. I sat in the stillness and whispered the hardest words I'd ever said: "God, I need help." That moment wasn't dramatic. There was no thunder, no light splitting the sky. Just me, twenty-eight years old, sitting in the dark, knees pulled to my chest, whispering a prayer I didn't even know how to form. I didn't grow up knowing what surrender looked like. I grew up around strong women who held it all together, even when the world crumbled around them. Crying meant weakness. Silence meant survival. Asking for help meant you'd already lost. So, when I said I didn't know how to give God control, it wasn't rebellion. It was fear disguised as pride. But fear was killing me.

That night, the weight of my years, the trauma, the failed relationships, the pretending, became unbearable. I remember staring at the ceiling, my thoughts a blur of exhaustion and regret. I wasn't suicidal, but I was tired of living like this. I was tired of the noise inside my own head, tired of running toward people who kept leaving me emptier than before. So, I did something that felt foreign: *I prayed*.

I wondered if God would even listen to someone like me, someone who had broken every promise, doubted His presence, and ignored His signs. Someone who had been so far from perfect, she questioned whether grace was still on the table. Still, I sat there, in the dark, in the quiet, on the edge of my bed, and began to speak to Him. I took a deep breath, lifted my head, and began to pray. I started small. No fancy words. No church tone. Just truth.

> "God, I don't even know if You're listening, but I can't do this anymore."

And then it poured out, all the pain, all the confusion, all the anger I'd been holding.

> "Where were you when I was hurting? Where were you when I was a child and couldn't understand why my body was no longer mine? Where were you when I kept choosing men who treated me like a placeholder? Why did I have to carry so much pain just to feel like I existed?"

My voice cracked under the weight of the questions I had never dared to ask. I felt foolish at first, like I was talking to the air. But as the words left my mouth, something in me softened. For the first time, I wasn't performing. I wasn't trying to sound strong. I wasn't trying to sound faithful. I was just being honest, broken, but honest. That night became the turning point. I didn't hear an audible voice, but I felt something stir in the quiet, a peace that didn't make sense. It was subtle, like a whisper beneath the chaos: "You're not alone." I cried until there were no tears left, and when I finally lay down, I felt lighter. Not healed but seen. It was the first night in years I didn't fall asleep to anxiety clawing at my chest.

In the days that followed, something began to shift. My heart wasn't instantly whole, but it was open. I started talking to God like I would a friend. At the grocery store. In the car. Folding laundry. He wasn't a faraway deity anymore; He was near, present in the smallest, most ordinary moments. He became the friend I didn't know I needed. And in the seasons to come, He would become the strength I didn't know I had. I was a blank canvas, wiped clean, and ready to paint a new life. Not one built on pain, but on purpose. And as I grew closer to Him, I began to notice something: my patterns started unraveling. I wasn't as quick to chase people. I stopped trying to prove my worth through busyness. I found myself craving solitude instead of attention.

Healing wasn't glamorous. It was quiet. It was humbling. It was days of crying and writing and deleting texts I shouldn't send. It was confronting truths I'd spent years avoiding. I realized that for most of my life, I had confused chaos for connection. I had called trauma chemistry. I had mistaken being needed for being loved. But that's not love. That's survival disguised as intimacy.

When I finally surrendered, I understood that God didn't want the version of me that had it all together. He wanted the real me, the one who was tired, lost, and full of doubt. Because that's the version He could work with. March 2014 became the month of my undoing and rebirth. One evening, I wrote down the prayer that changed my life. Not because I thought it was poetic, but because I didn't want to forget the moment I let go:

> "God, I don't know where to start, but thank you for listening to a girl like me. I've failed in every way possible. I've searched for love in all the wrong places. I've tried to control everything and broken everything in the process. I've doubted you, blamed you, and pushed you away. But I'm tired. I'm ready to surrender. Heal me. Teach me. Show me who I am without all this pain. And when you do, I'll do my part."

That night, I felt something break. It wasn't loud or visible. But inside, something shifted. It was like years of weight I didn't even realize I'd been carrying started to lift. I could finally breathe again.

Over the next few months, I started rebuilding, not from strength, but from surrender. I went back to church. I didn't go to be seen; I went to learn. I stopped numbing with alcohol. I stopped answering calls from people who only came around when they needed something. I started walking every morning, praying out loud, letting my thoughts unravel in conversation with God. That season taught me something powerful: transformation doesn't happen when life gets easier; it happens when you stop running from what hurts.

Forgiveness became the next lesson, and the hardest one. Forgiveness meant unpacking memories I had buried. It meant sitting with the truth that I had stayed in relationships that mirrored my trauma because they felt familiar. It meant acknowledging that I had been both the wounded and the wounder. I had hurt people, too, not intentionally, but because hurt people eventually leak their pain somewhere. Forgiving others was hard, but forgiving myself was harder. I had to learn to stop holding myself hostage to the woman I used to be. To stop replaying my mistakes like a movie on loop. To stop calling myself names, God never called me. I had to learn that grace isn't earned, it's received.

Forgiveness isn't about pretending something didn't happen. It's about choosing not to let it control you anymore. It's looking at the wound and saying, "You happened, but you won't define me." That realization changed how I saw everything, even my past. The pain didn't disappear, but it stopped feeling like punishment. It started to feel like preparation. Every heartbreak, every loss, every mistake was shaping me into someone more compassionate, more grounded, more aware.

Years later, in therapy, it taught me how to name my patterns, and faith taught me how to release them. I began to understand the psychological and spiritual connection between trauma and control. When you grow up in chaos, control becomes a coping mechanism. It's your way of creating safety where there was none. But control is exhausting. It keeps you hypervigilant, constantly anticipating the next hurt. What I learned in therapy is that surrender isn't weakness; it's regulation. It's allowing your nervous system to finally rest. That's what God was teaching me, not to stop caring, but to stop carrying everything alone.

There were days I stumbled. Days I doubted. Days I felt like I'd taken ten steps backward. But every time I wanted to give up, I'd remember how far I'd come, how I used to pray for the peace I now felt in moments of stillness. That's what healing looks like. Not perfection, but progress. Eventually, the metaphor made sense to me. I wasn't just rebuilding, I was becoming a blank canvas.

A blank canvas doesn't erase the artist's past; it holds the potential for what's next. It's the place where the Master Artist begins again, brushstroke by brushstroke, layer by layer. I wasn't starting over from nothing. I was starting over with everything I had learned. The brokenness, the lessons, the forgiveness, all of it became the texture beneath the new image being painted. For the first time, I wasn't chasing love. I was learning to embody it. I was learning to let my worth come from within, not from what someone else could give or take away. I began waking up with gratitude instead of anxiety. I stopped asking God to change my circumstances and started asking Him to change me. I no longer prayed for "the one." I prayed for wisdom, to recognize peace when it arrived, and to walk away when it didn't. That's what surrender looked like: less performing, more trusting. Less doing, more being. Less surviving, more living.

Healing didn't turn me into a saint. It turned me into someone self-aware enough to know when I was slipping back into old habits. It taught me to pause instead of reacting. To pray before I panic. To reflect before I repeat.

This chapter, transformation, wasn't about religion. It was about a relationship. About realizing that healing is both divine and deeply human. It's crying one day and laughing the next. It's forgiving yourself for not knowing better and committing to do better now. And that's what being a blank canvas means: choosing to be open again.

Open to joy. Open to peace. Open to love that doesn't require self-abandonment.

When I look back on that version of me, the one who sat on the edge of the bed in March 2014, I want to hug her. I want to tell her she wasn't crazy, she wasn't too much, and she wasn't broken beyond repair. She was simply unfinished. And now, years later, I finally understand that God doesn't waste pain. He repurposes it. Every scar becomes a brushstroke. Every tear becomes water in His paint. And what He's creating is something beautiful, not despite the brokenness, but because of it.

So, if you've ever reached the end of yourself, I want you to know that's not the end. That's the beginning. You are not too far gone. You are not unworthy of love. You are not beyond redemption. You are a blank canvas, waiting for your next masterpiece.

Therapist's Work For The Reader: The New Me

What would surrender look like for you if you finally stopped trying to control everything?

- What would it sound like?
- What would it feel like in your body to finally trust God with the parts of you that still feel too broken to name?
- What pain are you still trying to manage in your own strength?
- Where have you confused control with safety?

And if you're really honest,

- Have you made room for healing, or have you just gotten good at hiding?

Starting over becomes difficult when you realize you must unlearn who you were taught to be.

Chapter 8

Closed For Business

"Sometimes the safest thing you can do is stop loving people for who you hope they'll become and start responding to who they already are."

There comes a point when you get tired of bleeding for things that never loved you back. That was where I found myself, not angry, not bitter, just done. Done with temporary affection that left permanent bruises. Done confusing pleasure for purpose. Done leaving the door wide open for men who never had the decency to knock. Sex had been my drug of choice, the counterfeit comfort I ran to when I didn't want to face myself. For years, it was how I softened the loneliness and silenced the parts of me I didn't know how to heal. But standing in the wreckage of everything it had cost me, I finally saw the truth: I couldn't keep living like that.

For most of my life, I tied sex to identity. If a man desired me, I felt worthy. If he stayed afterward, I felt chosen. If he came back, I felt valuable. But none of it was real. What I was chasing wasn't pleasure; it was validation. I wanted to be seen. I wanted someone's touch to tell me I mattered. When I didn't feel that in everyday life, I looked for it in bedrooms. I mistook chemistry for compatibility and intensity for intimacy. I believed sex was love because my early life didn't teach me other ways to recognize connection. And each time the relationship fell apart, I blamed myself for not being enough to make him stay.

Eventually, sex became a performance. A currency. A negotiation. I offered my body, hoping it would earn me affection or commitment. If I pleased him enough, maybe he would choose me. That logic only works in fairytales and trauma bonds. In real life, it left me emptier after every encounter. I wasn't offering myself from a place of wholeness; I was offering from a wound. And wounds don't build intimacy. They only bleed on people who didn't cut you.

Looking back now, I can see the pattern clearly. I overlooked red flags if the sex was good. I confused passion with connection. If I felt butterflies, I assumed it was fate, when really, it was anxiety. My body had normalized dysfunction for so long that I could no longer tell the difference between being excited and being on edge. That's the dangerous thing about trauma: it can shape your preferences without your consent. You start craving what hurts you because it's familiar. And familiarity can feel like love when you've never experienced love without pain.

After the last relationship, I knew something had to change. For real this time. I couldn't keep trading sacred pieces of myself for temporary comfort. I couldn't keep bypassing emotional work by using my body as a shortcut to closeness. So I did something that, years earlier, would've sounded unrealistic for someone like me: I closed up shop.

Sex was off the table, not because I believed it was wrong, but because I finally admitted that I wasn't handling it in a healthy way. I wasn't choosing sex; I was using it. Using it to self-medicate. Using it to outrun loneliness. Using it as a substitute for conversations I wasn't brave enough to have. I didn't need to be touched; I needed to be healed.

At first, celibacy felt like withdrawal. Not because I missed sex, but because I missed what it represented. I missed feeling desirable. I missed the illusion of control I felt when I could make a man melt. I missed the temporary numbness that came after the high. But the more honest I became with myself, the clearer it became that what I had called "empowerment" was actually survival. I had been performing *confidence* while silently negotiating with shame.

Choosing celibacy wasn't about deprivation; it was about detox. For years, I had used sexual intimacy like anesthesia, numbing pain I didn't know how to name. But healing doesn't happen in avoidance. It happens in the quiet, in the space between the distractions, in the moments where you finally sit still long enough to hear yourself think.

Those first weeks were humbling. I deleted numbers. Blocked old flings. Turned down those late-night invitations that read, "You up?" Turned off the TV when scenes became too triggering. I unfollowed accounts that fed my fantasies. I began treating my boundaries like rituals, intentional, sacred, non-negotiable. The hardest part wasn't abstaining; it was facing the silence sex had been covering for years. And in that silence, I started to see the truth behind my patterns.

Sexual trauma, especially childhood trauma, distorts how you inhabit your body and how you experience intimacy.[15] [16] Some respond by shutting down completely. Others, like me, respond by leaning in too far, too fast, too often. I didn't sleep with men because I was liberated. I slept with them because I was trying to reclaim power. Because if I initiated it, I could pretend I wasn't being used. Because if I gave my body willingly, maybe it would erase the memory of when it wasn't mine to give. But choice without healing is still bondage. It just looks more sophisticated.

When your body has been a battleground, you learn to mistake intensity for connection. You confuse chaos with chemistry. You chase reenactments of your wounds, trying to master them this time. You call it love, so the pain feels purposeful. That's how trauma tricks you: it convinces you to seek what once harmed you, hoping this time it will heal instead.

Celibacy forced me to break that cycle. Not because it is the only way to heal, but because it was the way I needed to heal. I treated my body like a home instead of a transaction. I learned the difference between desire, compulsion, attachment, and avoidance. I learned how to feel without performing. How to want without abandoning myself. How to connect without confusing proximity for intimacy.

The first few months were brutal. Loneliness does not leave quietly; it puts up a fight. My phone would buzz, and I'd feel that old pull, the impulse to respond, to engage, to negotiate a boundary I had just set. Sometimes I'd scroll through old photos. Sometimes I almost texted someone

---

[15] Brown, Whitney. "Shattered Innocence, Scarred Love: A Phenomenological Study on the Effects of Childhood Sexual Abuse of African American Women on their Romantic Relationships." Order No. 31937022, University of Holy Cross, 2025. https://uhcno.idm.oclc.org/login?url=https://www.proquest.com/dissertations-theses/shattered-innocence-scarred-love-phenomenological/docview/3201918934/se-2.

[16] Cindy M Meston, Alessandra H Rellini, and Julia R Heiman, "Women's History of Sexual Abuse, Their Sexuality, and Sexual Self-schemas.," *Journal of Consulting and Clinical Psychology* 74, no. 2 (April 1, 2006): 229–36, https://doi.org/10.1037/0022-006x.74.2.229.

from my past. But each time, I remembered the mornings I woke up hollow. The nights I cried in silence. The way I'd stare at the ceiling, wondering why I felt smaller after every encounter.

I refused to go back there.

As time passed, something unexpected happened: I began to feel at home in my own skin. My mind became clearer. My standards rose. My discernment sharpened. I began noticing things I had once ignored: the inconsistencies and intentions. I stopped shrinking to be chosen. I stopped negotiating with my worth. I stopped confusing attention for affection. Silence became nourishing instead of intimidating. Celibacy stopped feeling like a restriction and started feeling like freedom.

I found new rituals. Journaling at night. Prayer in the morning. Walks without music. Deep breaths before responding to old triggers. I learned what peace actually felt like, slow, steady, grounding, the opposite of the adrenaline spikes I once called passion.

There were moments I doubted myself. Holidays where the loneliness felt louder. Nights where my old coping mechanisms whispered familiar lies. But every time I was tempted to break my commitment, I remembered what it cost me the last time I settled. Eventually, I stopped worrying about how long I would remain celibate. I wasn't waiting on a man; I was waiting on clarity. I was waiting on the version of myself who knew she deserved more. I was waiting for peace, reciprocity, consistency, and emotional safety. And until those things came, the door to my body remained closed, not out of fear, but out of reverence. I closed for business because I finally understood the value of what was inside.

I stopped renting out rooms in my soul to people who didn't plan to stay. I stopped letting men audition for roles I no longer needed them to play. I locked the door, not to keep love out, but to give it a chance to grow roots in me first. For the first time in my life, I understood that wholeness was never about being touched. It was about finally feeling at home in my own skin. And that, more than anything, is what changed me.

When The Body Remembers What The Mind Tries To Forget

There's something sobering about arriving at the moment when you can no longer lie to yourself. When the loud, familiar narratives you've used as excuses, the ones shaped by fatherlessness, abandonment, early wounds, and survival, stop working. When you realize that the story you've been telling about why you choose the relationships you choose no longer holds up against the truth staring back at you. For a long time, I believed that my history justified my patterns. That my trauma explained my choices. The absence of a father meant I would always crave someone to choose me, even if it meant shrinking to fit inside their neglect. But eventually, that reasoning becomes too small to carry the weight of the life you want to build.

Closing myself off sexually wasn't just about my body; it was about my story. For years, sex was the place where I rehearsed every unanswered question from childhood. Am I wanted? Am I enough? Will someone stay? Will someone choose me? My body became the stage where I reenacted my losses, one encounter at a time. And the frightening part is that I couldn't see it. I called it empowerment, adulthood, liberation. But really, it was coping. It was grief in disguise. It was me trying to use pleasure to fill the father-shaped emptiness that lived in the center of my heart.

Trauma has a way of convincing you that the familiar is safe. Even when the familiar is harmful. You reach for the same types of people, the same intensity, the same patterns, not because you don't know better, but because your nervous system has been trained to mistake anxiety for excitement. Longing becomes synonymous with love. Distance becomes a cue for pursuit. The absence you were raised in becomes the blueprint for every attachment that follows. That's the part people don't talk about. Desire is not always rooted in preference. Sometimes it is rooted in pain. And if you never stop to examine the source, the repetition feels inevitable.

But there comes a moment that interrupts everything. A moment when you realize you're not just tired, you're empty. Not just hurt, you're hollow. Not just disappointed, you're done. My moment came when I realized I had been outsourcing my worth for years. Trading access to my body in hopes that someone would confirm what I couldn't believe about myself. I wasn't seeking intimacy; I was seeking identity. I wanted someone to tell me I mattered because I hadn't yet learned how to believe it alone.

When I chose celibacy, people assumed it was about morality or religion. But it was about reclamation. It was the moment I told every earlier version of me, every scared little girl, every heartbroken teenager, every twenty-something desperate for love, that she no longer had to earn her place in someone's life. That she no longer had to beg or bargain for affection. That her worth wasn't located in someone else's hands. Choosing myself required more courage than choosing a man ever did.

Celibacy stripped away the noise. Without sex as a shortcut to connection, I had to confront the parts of me I had avoided. The loneliness I had outrun. The shame I had masked with confidence. The unhealed grief of a father's absence that I had tried to silence by being wanted. When the distractions fell away, I finally heard the truth my trauma had been shouting for years: I had been feeling people to avoid feeling my own wounds.

There is nothing glamorous about that realization. It is painful. It is humbling. It strips away the excuses and confronts you with the version of yourself that you avoided for years. The version of yourself that smiles through heartbreak. The version of yourself that says you are fine while you are falling apart. The version of yourself that believes the only thing you have to offer is your body. Celibacy did not make me holy. It made me aware. It made me sit in the discomfort long enough to understand it. It made me trace my patterns back to their source.

Healing isn't soft work. It is an excavation. It is dismantling the narratives that once protected you but now imprison you. It is admitting that what you called attraction was sometimes reenactment. What you called chemistry was often anxiety. That which you called love was, in hindsight, a negotiation with abandonment.

But healing is also choosing differently. For me, that choice began with closing the doors that had always been too easy to open. It meant drawing a line between desire and self-destruction. Between being seen and being valued. Between being wanted and being loved.

And as the months passed, something unexpected happened: I met myself. Not the version I performed. Not the version broken men shaped. Not the version trauma held captive. But the woman beneath all of that. The woman who had been waiting for me to choose her.

This reflection exists for her. For me. And for every woman who has ever tried to use her body to answer a question only healing can resolve. You don't break patterns by willpower alone. You break them by telling the truth. And the truth is this: you deserve love that does not require you to abandon yourself to receive it.

Closing for business wasn't a shutdown. It was a reopening. A rebuilding. A return to myself. A declaration that my body, my peace, and my story are no longer available for discount. And when I finally understood that something sacred had happened, wholeness no longer felt like a possibility. It felt like a promise.

Chapter 9

Revelations

"Everything will finally make sense when you understand that your pain was an experience, not your identity."

As I began writing this book, I found myself sitting in the wreckage of my own story, not metaphorically, but tangibly. My life had unraveled in ways I hadn't fully acknowledged until I started putting pen to paper. The pain was layered, the lessons were loud, and the truth was unavoidable. Inside that unraveling, something sacred emerged. I began to see patterns I had grown used to calling "normal" and how grace had been quietly working behind the scenes of even my worst decisions. What I once called detours, I now recognize as divine redirection. What I used to label as failure, I began to interpret as a form of formation. Slowly, I started to understand that my life wasn't just a sequence of random, chaotic events; it was a map being drawn by something greater than me, even when I didn't know where I was going. The mess was not just mine; it was inherited. The revelation, though, was mine to claim.

Nothing in my life began to make sense until I made the conscious decision to interrogate not just my behaviors, but the beliefs that shaped them. The work of transformation isn't about surface-level change; it's about getting underneath the habits, the coping, the reactions, and uncovering the systems that taught us how to survive. Let's be clear: dysfunction doesn't appear out of nowhere. It is passed down, packaged as strength, and dressed in the language of love, culture, tradition, and even religion. We are often socialized to normalize what should never have been acceptable. We are taught to be strong before we're allowed to be soft, to perform perfection before we understand peace. Many of us learned early on that silence was safer than truth, and that survival was the only thing we could afford. But survival is not the same as wholeness. And silence does not protect us; it just prolongs our suffering.

Revelation didn't arrive kindly. It was disruptive, loud, unforgiving. It stripped away excuses and surfaced truths I did not want to hold. It revealed how deeply I had been shaped by things I never consented to. It showed me how my childhood was not just a memory; it was a foundation. The more I peeled back the layers, the more I realized that healing would require more than acknowledgment. It would require unlearning, reparenting, accountability, and radical self-trust. Revelation gave me language for what I had been living without definition. It helped me connect the dots between my past and my present so I could begin building a new future. It also made something clear: my pain might not have been my choice, but my healing had to be.

So in this final chapter, I want to share some of the most defining revelations that reshaped how I see myself, how I give and receive love, and how I began building a life rooted in wholeness instead of survival. I offer them to you as invitations, not instructions, as truths earned through loss, therapy, grace, and surrender. If they find you, I hope they free you. Let's begin.

Revelation 1: You Are Not Responsible For What Broke You, But You Are Responsible For What You Build Next

There is a shift that happens when you realize the pain you have been carrying your whole life was never yours to begin with. You wake up one day and start to question why you flinch at love, why you over-explain when you say no, or why you shrink when you should be shining. For many of us, we inherited trauma like old furniture: heavy, worn, but too familiar to throw out. We were raised in homes where silence was mistaken for peace, where survival was praised but emotional safety was never discussed. Some of us were taught that strength meant suffering quietly. That love meant staying loyal, even when it hurt. That boundaries were disrespectful, and voicing your needs was a luxury we could not afford. We accepted those rules as truth, not because they made sense, but because we were too young to know any better. We did not write the script, but we were expected to perform it perfectly and without complaint. But adulthood eventually puts a mirror in front of you.

One of the hardest truths I have had to accept is that healing is my job. It does not matter who dropped the ball, who failed me, or who taught me how to love in broken ways. At some point, I had to decide what to do with the pieces. That is what this revelation is about. It is not about blaming your parents, your past, or your pain. It is about reclaiming your power to build something different. You are not responsible for the trauma that shaped you, but you are responsible for interrupting the pattern. That is the part no one wants to hear. Because healing is not romantic. It is messy. It forces you to revisit moments you swore you buried. It asks you to question what you were taught, to hold space for the version of you that survived, and to still believe in the version that is trying to thrive. If I am honest, it is exhausting sometimes. But the reward is this: you stop living like you are always in survival mode. You begin to feel like you belong in your own body. You start showing up for yourself in ways you never knew were possible. That is the real work, choosing yourself every day, even when your past trained you not to.

Healing is not about forgetting what happened. It is about learning to live beyond it. It is about refusing to let the worst parts of your story become the loudest. For women especially, this work is profound. We have been conditioned to inherit responsibility that never belonged to us and to carry burdens that were never ours to lift. However, generational pain cannot be healed through martyrdom. We do not have to keep bleeding from wounds we did not create. We get to say: this ends with me. That is what this revelation gave me: the permission to put some things down. To say, yes, I was hurt. Yes, I was shaped by things beyond my control. But now that I know better, I get to do better. That is what accountability looks like on this side of healing. It is not about shame; it is about choice. It is about deciding what kind of legacy you want to leave behind, not just for your kids, but for yourself. You deserve peace, softness, and to become someone you are proud of. No, it is not easy, but staying stuck in pain you did not cause will not make it any easier. At some point, you have to stop waiting for the apology that may never come and start giving yourself the closure you have always deserved.

Revelation 2: You Can't Heal In The Same Environment That Made You Sick

There comes a time when you have to stop watering dead soil. Many of us remain rooted in environments, whether it is family, friendships, churches, or romantic relationships, that repeatedly invalidate our worth and then wonder why our healing never takes root. Here is the hard truth: you cannot grow in spaces that demand your silence, question your boundaries, or see your self-awareness as rebellion.

For a long time, I believed my healing would just appear inside the same rooms where I had been broken. I thought if I loved harder, prayed more, explained myself better, and proved my loyalty long enough, the spaces that hurt me would eventually turn into places that healed me. I sincerely believed I could transform environments by losing more and more of myself inside them. But what I did not realize is that healing is not just an internal shift. It is deeply environmental.

Some of us are trying to recover while still living in the very conditions that made us sick in the first place. We sit at tables where our boundaries are laughed at, where our truth is dismissed as disrespect, and where any attempt to change the rules is treated as rebellion. Then we wonder why our healing will not stick. You cannot grow in soil that resists your roots.

This is especially true in many of our communities, where leaving harmful environments is often labeled betrayal instead of survival. Within Black families, friend groups, and faith spaces, loyalty is sometimes measured by how much you can endure without complaint. You are praised for staying, even when staying is slowly destroying you. You are celebrated for being "strong," even when that strength is just another name for tolerated harm.

For years, I tried to heal in environments that refused to acknowledge the harm they caused. I wanted the people who hurt me to also witness my transformation. I wanted them to clap for the healed version of me, but they never made room for it. So I stayed. I tried to negotiate with dysfunction. I spiritualized my suffering and called it faith. I confused proximity with connection and silence with peace. But the truth is simple, even if it hurts: you cannot build a new life inside an old wound.

Healing requires boundaries, and boundaries often require distance. That distance might be emotional, physical, spiritual, or all three. It might mean limiting conversations with a parent who still gaslights you, stepping back from a friendship that only survives through gossip and shared pain, or leaving a church that preaches shame in the name of love. It is not about cutting people off out of bitterness; it is about choosing peace over perpetual harm. And for many of us, especially where loyalty is often mistaken for love and tradition is rarely questioned, this revelation can feel like a betrayal. But it is not. It is liberation. You do not owe your healing to people who harmed you. You do not have to stay loyal to dysfunction just because you were raised in it. There is no badge of honor in continuing to breathe in toxicity just because you have built a life around it. Your healing deserves better soil. And sometimes, the bravest thing you will ever do is walk away from what you once called home.

Revelation 3: Healing Requires Telling The Truth About Yourself

Accountability is one of the most avoided and misunderstood practices in healing. Somewhere along the way, it became entangled with shame, punishment, and blame. We are taught to associate it with getting in trouble, with being wrong, with being exposed. But real accountability is not about guilt; it is about growth. It is the recognition that while you did not choose your trauma, you do decide how long you let it lead your life. It is not about blaming yourself for the wound; it is about deciding who gets to hold the knife next. Without accountability, healing becomes a passive hope rather than an active pursuit. You cannot transform what you will not take ownership of.

In my work as a therapist, I have seen the way clients sidestep this truth, not because they are lazy, but because they are afraid. Afraid that if they admit the role they have played, they will confirm every terrible thing someone once said about them. Afraid that their pain will be minimized or dismissed. However, the truth is that accountability does not invalidate your story; it empowers you within it. It says, "Yes, this happened to me, and now I choose what happens next." That is where real power begins. Because staying in the role of the wounded might feel justified, but it keeps you waiting for someone else to come and make it right. And often, they never do. Healing requires active participation. It calls for you to move beyond what happened to you and ask, What am I doing with the pain now that I know it is there?

For me, accountability did not come easily. I fought it. I blamed everyone who had failed me, and truthfully, some of them deserved the blame. But I reached a point where blame stopped being useful. It did not help me sleep better. It did not help me stop crying. It did not keep me from repeating the same cycles with different people. I had to look at myself, not to shame myself, but to save myself. I had to admit that I had stayed too long in places that diminished me. I ignored red flags because I did not want to be alone. I mistook attention for love, silence for peace, and struggle for purpose. And while I did not create the pain I inherited, I had made choices that deepened it. That realization did not destroy me; it awakened me. I could not keep calling everything a betrayal when, in truth, I was betraying myself too.

Owning my part was not just about failed relationships. It was about the way I avoided discomfort by pretending everything was fine. The way I numbed myself with distractions instead of sitting with my feelings. The way I silenced my intuition just to keep the peace. I had to get radically honest about how often I prioritized being chosen over being cherished. About how I confused sacrifice with loyalty. Accountability required me to ask questions that stripped away my defenses: Why do I tolerate what I say I do not want? What am I afraid I will have to face if I let this go? What version of myself am I still protecting, even though she no longer serves me? Those questions did not feel good, but they set me free. Because when you tell the whole truth, you stop editing your story to make yourself more palatable. You start healing in a way that is sustainable, not performative.

True accountability is a lifestyle. It shows up in how you speak to others, how you handle conflict, and how you sit with your discomfort instead of projecting it. It is present when you pause before reacting, when you ask yourself if the story you are telling is honest or just convenient. It is in the willingness to call yourself out before the world has to. No matter your background, your culture, or your past, learning to take full ownership of your healing is the difference between repeating your pain and rising from it. This is not about perfection; it is about courage. The courage to stop rehearsing your suffering and start rewriting your story. Accountability is not a punishment. It is a portal, one that leads you back to your power, your peace, and ultimately, your purpose.

Revelation 4: Not Everything Deserves A Seat At The Table Of Your Life

Letting go sounds simple until it is your turn to do it. Until you are staring at the thing, the person, the situation, the identity you once prayed for, realizing that holding on is no longer worth it. I did not understand this at first. I used to believe letting go was synonymous with quitting, that walking away meant I failed, or that I was not strong enough to stick it out. But in time, life humbled me. It taught me that holding on out of obligation is not loyalty; it is fear in disguise. Sometimes we do not hold on because we love the person or the pattern. We hold on because we are afraid of who we will be without it. But healing invites us to confront that fear and ask ourselves: What am I sacrificing to maintain what no longer serves me?

From a clinical perspective, many of us are neurologically wired to cling to what is familiar, even if it is harmful. This is especially true for those of us with trauma histories. If you grew up in a home where love was inconsistent, conditional, or confused with control, your nervous system may associate chaos with connection. It is not your fault; it is biology. Your body learned to survive the storm, so now it searches for thunder in every quiet room. That is why letting go does not just feel like a choice; it feels like a betrayal of your past, your family, your younger self. However, what I have come to learn, both through my healing and in the healing work I do with clients, is this: growth always feels like loss at first. Because it is a loss, the loss of who you were, the identity you built around surviving instead of thriving. That grief is valid, but it does not mean you are making the wrong decision. It means you are making a new one.

Letting go is not passive; it is intentional. It is an active reclamation of your life, your peace, and your worth. It often comes at a high emotional cost. You may feel guilt, doubt yourself, romanticize the past, or believe the narrative that you are the one who changed for the worse. But here is what I want you to remember: not everything that starts with love ends with purpose. Some relationships expire because they were only meant to teach you who you no longer want to be. If you continue holding on, you will end up resenting the very thing you once cherished. And I guarantee you this: staying in a dynamic that drains you just to avoid guilt is a form of emotional self-harm. When we do that, we are not being loyal; we are being complicit in our own pain. You cannot heal in the same environment that made you sick. You cannot become whole while holding on to what was only ever meant to be a lesson.

My revelation about letting go did not arrive gently; it dragged me through every emotion I tried to suppress. There were things I had to release that I still loved. People I had to walk away from who never apologized. Versions of myself I had to bury, not because they were bad, but because they could no longer carry the weight of my healing. What I have realized is that letting go is a form of self-respect. It is saying, "I may have tolerated this before, but I know better now." It is choosing your wholeness over their comfort. And yes, it is hard. But it is the kind of hard that frees you. It is the kind of hard that reintroduces you to yourself.

Sometimes, the most revolutionary thing we can do is choose ourselves in a world that taught us self-abandonment. Letting go is not always dramatic. Sometimes it is quiet, a shift in posture, a canceled call, or a boundary held firm. But do not mistake that quiet for weakness. It takes strength to release what once felt like everything. It takes clarity to walk away from cycles that once defined you. It takes courage to believe that peace is possible on the other side of pain. Letting go is not the loss; it is the liberation. It is the moment we decide that our healing matters more than their comfort, our growth more than their approval. And when we finally put down what was never ours to carry, we do not just feel relief, we find resurrection. This is where we begin again, lighter, wiser, and no longer afraid to choose ourselves.

Revelation 5: Being Chosen Is Not The Same As Being Valued

One of the most sobering truths I had to face in my healing journey was this: being chosen does not always mean you are being loved, seen, or valued. In fact, many of us have been chosen by people who did not have the capacity to honor our presence, only to use it for their own comfort, control, or convenience. We were chosen to be the strong one in the family, the dependable friend, the overachiever at work, the loyal partner. But when you are picked for your performance rather than your personhood, that is not love. That is functional attachment, and it leaves a deep imprint on the psyche, one that can make us believe we have to earn our place in every room we enter.

This lesson did not start in adulthood. It began in childhood, in the subtle and not-so-subtle ways our caregivers taught us what earned their attention. Maybe you were the "golden child," the one who did everything right because your parents needed someone to shine. Or maybe you were the emotional caretaker, the one your mother leaned on instead of protecting. You were chosen, yes, but not seen for your needs. You were assigned a role, not embraced as a whole person. And so, the story began: I am worthy when I perform. I am loved when I over-function. I am valuable when I abandon myself to meet others' expectations.

We carry those early assignments into every other domain of life, romantic relationships, friendships, workplaces, and even faith communities. We find ourselves in dynamics where we are constantly picked but rarely protected. We become the go-to person, the fix-it friend, the reliable employee, the forgiving sibling. And the worst part is this: we think that being chosen in these ways is evidence of our worth. But it is not. It is evidence that people have gotten used to taking from us without learning how to truly hold us. Eventually, our bodies start to protest. Burnout, anxiety, depression, and chronic resentment set in. Our nervous systems sound the alarm. But we often ignore the signal because we mistake exhaustion for connection, and we do not know what value, real value, looks like when it is not attached to struggle. These are not just emotional reactions; they are trauma responses rooted in our attachment systems.

From a clinical lens, this is often rooted in anxious-preoccupied or disorganized attachment styles, formed in environments where love was inconsistent, conditional, or unavailable. These wounds teach us to equate emotional labor with belonging. So we people-please, overperform, and tolerate mistreatment just to avoid rejection. And here is the hardest part: when you have been chosen for your function, real love can feel boring, foreign, or even threatening. Because it does not activate your survival system, it invites your authenticity. And for many of us, that feels unsafe.

But here is where it gets complicated: many of us carry these wounds into our romantic relationships, unaware that we are still trying to earn value by being chosen. We chase validation from partners who mirror our earliest attachments, not because it is healthy, but because it is familiar. If we were taught that love must be earned through self-sacrifice, we would unconsciously seek out lovers who make us prove our worth. If we were raised to perform for connection, we will mistake emotional labor for intimacy. And when a relationship starts to feel one-sided or unbalanced, we often do not leave; we double down, trying harder, giving more, hoping that being chosen again will finally feel like being cherished. This dynamic is especially painful because it convinces us to stay in emotionally unavailable partnerships, mistaking breadcrumbs for nourishment. But the truth is this: your ability to be chosen has never been the problem. The real question is, are you being valued when you are not performing?

So what does it mean to be valued? It means being seen beyond your usefulness. It means existing in spaces where you are allowed to rest, to receive, to be flawed and still loved. It means people recognize your boundaries, not just your bandwidth. It means you are not just selected when someone needs something; you are invested in, even when you have nothing left to give. When I finally started recognizing that distinction in my own life, I grieved. I had to grieve the spaces that could not hold me, even though I held them for years. I had to let go of friendships that only reached out to me when they needed healing. I had to detach from family roles that silenced me to keep others comfortable. I had to stop proving and start preserving. Because being chosen is not the same as being loved, not when that choice asks you to abandon yourself. Sometimes, the most revolutionary thing we can do is choose ourselves in a world that taught us self-abandonment is okay.

Revelation 6: She Kept Me Alive, But She Can't Take Me Any Further

I remember sitting in my car after another long day of pretending. I had just left a dinner where I smiled through stories I did not enjoy and held space for people who never held any for me. I drove home in silence, pulled into the driveway, turned off the engine, and just sat there, too exhausted to move, too numb to cry. My body was not just tired; it was speaking. My chest was tight, my jaw clenched, my hands trembling slightly from what I now know was nervous system fatigue. I had been carrying too much for too long. In that stillness, a thought came so clearly it felt like someone else had spoken it: She kept you alive, but she can't take you any further.

I knew exactly who she was. She was the version of me that learned how to survive. The one who did not cry so she would not be labeled weak. The one who worked twice as hard to be half as valued. The one who made herself useful so she would not be discarded. She was sharp, intuitive, always anticipating other people's needs, hypervigilant, and endlessly self-sacrificing. She knew how to read a room, how to silence her voice, how to function in chaos, and how to become whatever others needed to feel safe.

She was my armor, my mask, and for years, she protected me in environments that did not know how to love me. She kept me alive. But that armor came with a cost. It kept the danger out, yes, but it also kept the love out. It kept me from being hurt, but also from being held. It guarded me from abandonment, but at the expense of connection. While she got me through the darkest chapters of my life, I had come to a point in my healing where survival alone was no longer enough. I did not want to just make it; I wanted to live. I wanted to be seen. I wanted softness. But she did not know how to live in a world where vulnerability was not a threat. She only knew how to survive in one where it was.

When you grow up in survival mode, whether because of trauma, neglect, abandonment, or environments that never nurtured your emotional needs, you build an identity around staying safe, not around being seen. You become hyper-independent, hyper-aware, hypervigilant. The tricky part is, people often praise that version of you. They call you strong, resilient, and reliable, but they rarely ask what it costs you to become that way. No one sees the little girl who never got to rest. The woman who never got to choose softness because life demanded steel. We do not question the armor until it starts suffocating us, until it becomes harder to breathe inside the persona than outside it.

In therapy, this is what we often refer to as the adaptive self or the protector part in internal family systems (IFS) therapy. These parts of us emerge during times of threat or emotional chaos. They are not flaws; they are strategies. Strategies developed in childhood or early adulthood to keep us safe, to ensure belonging, to manage abandonment, or to earn conditional love. While these parts serve us well during traumatic or unstable seasons, they can become barriers when we transition into safer, more secure spaces. That same vigilance that kept us protected becomes the thing that keeps us disconnected. The very survival skills that once saved our lives begin to sabotage our peace.

What is more, many people, especially those with complex trauma or disorganized attachment, mistake the survival self for the authentic self. We become so fused with this hyper-independent, emotionally armored identity that we do not recognize who we are without the struggle. But healing requires that separation. It requires us to grieve the old roles we played, the old selves we inhabited, and the emotional protections we once needed. In therapeutic terms, we begin to identify with adaptive identity restructuring when the self you constructed to survive no longer fits the life you want to build. I had to learn that I was not betraying her by evolving. I was honoring her by finally taking us someplace safe and teaching her that she no longer had to drive the car. That we now get to live from a place of choice, not just instinct. She had done her job, and beautifully so, but healing demanded a new version of me. One that could live in rest, in joy, and in trust. And the truth is, the life I was trying to build, the intimacy I wanted to experience, the peace I was seeking, could not coexist with the armor I was still wearing. And that is what healing is: not shaming the parts that helped us survive, but thanking them, and then showing them what it means to truly live.

Revelation 7: Peace Doesn't Just Happen, You Have To Cultivate It

I used to think peace was something that just happened, something that would show up once the chaos stopped, the people changed, or life finally "got it together." But healing taught me that peace is not a reward for endurance. It is a practice, a decision, something you build and protect, not something you sit around waiting for. For a long time, I thought I had peace simply because things were quiet, but what I had was silence. And there is a difference. Silence can still feel tense. It can still feel unsafe. Peace, on the other hand, is a felt sense of safety. It is when your mind, your body, and your spirit finally exhale together and work in unison.

When I started removing the chaos from my life, walking away from unhealthy relationships, establishing boundaries, and being more intentional with my energy, I expected to feel better right away. But what actually happened was increased confusion, discomfort, and an odd kind of emptiness. That emptiness made me question if I had made the right decisions to embark on this journey. But the truth is, I was detoxing. I was coming down from years of emotional overstimulation. My nervous system was used to being on high alert, and when things got calm, it did not feel good; it felt unfamiliar. That was the moment I realized I did not know what peace felt like. I had been in fight-or-flight for so long that stillness felt like danger.

This is a common response for people who have lived in survival mode. Whether you experienced trauma, abandonment, instability, or chronic stress, your body learns to normalize that state. You begin to associate tension with connection. You mistake adrenaline for excitement. You confuse control with safety. When those objects are removed, your body interprets calm as suspicious. When we live outside of our window of tolerance for long periods, our bodies adapt, but those adaptations do not always serve us in healthy environments. So when peace finally enters the picture, we do not feel safe; we feel disoriented.

Cultivating peace meant I had to rewire my response to calm. I had to stop seeing peace as boring or unproductive. I had to retrain my body to rest without guilt. I had to learn that being still did not mean being lazy. That quiet did not mean something was wrong. That no one texting me back right away was not a sign I was being abandoned. I had to check the stories I was telling myself and question whether they were grounded in fear or in reality. That is what the work of cultivating peace looks like. It is not about burning sage and buying journals. It is about doing the daily, sometimes uncomfortable work of teaching your mind and body that you are no longer in danger, even if your trauma still tries to convince you otherwise.

Peace also meant learning to stop letting people steal my energy. It meant being okay with disappointing others if it meant preserving myself. It meant understanding that overstimulation was not a badge of honor, and burnout was not proof that I cared. I had to stop glorifying chaos and start building a life that felt like ease, not because everything was perfect, but because I had created enough stability within myself to stay grounded no matter what was happening around me. Peace is not the absence of hard things. It is the presence of a nervous system that knows how to return to safety even when hard things come. That is when I knew I had finally shifted. I did not panic when things got calm. I did not seek dysfunction just to feel needed. I did not crave the high of being overstretched. I started choosing peace on purpose, and that changed everything.

Most of what weighs a person down was learned long before they realized they had a choice.

Epilogue

What Came After

 I thought that once I found peace, the hard part would be over. That if I did the work, faced the trauma, told the truth, and took accountability, then I could finally exhale and be free. And for a while, I was. There was this stillness I had never known. Not quite like silence, but quiet like safety. My mind wasn't racing. My body wasn't bracing for the next betrayal. I had never experienced peace like that before: real, embodied, soul-level peace. But what no one tells you is that peace comes with a price. Once you've tasted it, everything not aligned with it becomes unbearable. The people you loved might not recognize you anymore. The spaces you once tolerated will start to feel like cages. The parts of you who survived dysfunction will panic when they realize the chaos is gone. And then comes the test. Not one single test, but waves of moments that whisper, sometimes scream: Will you go back to who you were, or will you choose who you're becoming?

I wish I could say I always chose well after this, because I didn't. I failed some of those tests. I clung to people I should have released. I broke my own boundaries to avoid being the villain in someone else's story. I slipped back into old habits because they felt familiar, predictable, safe in the way a storm can feel safe when you've lived your whole life inside of one. But even in those failures, I learned. Even in the setbacks, something sacred was being revealed. Peace, I learned, isn't a destination. It's a practice. A discipline. And sometimes the most painful part of growth is realizing you prayed for transformation but weren't prepared for everything it would require.

This book captures the beginning of my healing, the season where the light first broke through. These were the truths that surfaced in my twenties, during a time when I genuinely believed I had life figured out. But healing isn't linear, and neither is living. My thirties ushered in a deeper unraveling: a grief I wasn't expecting, losses I never imagined I'd have to hold, and lessons that didn't simply nudge me forward; they confronted me. They cut. They reshaped. They demanded a kind of honesty I had spent years avoiding. That part of the story? The part where peace is tested, and everything you've healed from gets called back to the surface. That's a story for another time. And I'll tell it. One day in the next book.

Appendix

Resources For Help

If this book has brought up painful memories, emotional discomfort, or a desire for support, you do not have to navigate that alone. The following resources may offer help:

Therapy Support and Search Tools

- PsychologyToday.com
- TherapyForBlackGirls.com
- MentalHealthMatch.com

Crisis Support Services

- National Suicide & Crisis Lifeline: 988 or 1-800-273-8255
- SAMHSA National Helpline: 1-800-662-HELP (4357)
- NAMI (National Alliance on Mental Illness) Text NAMI to 741741
- STAR (Sexual, Trauma, Awareness, and Response) 24/7 hotline 1-855-435-7827
- RAINN (Rape, Abuse, and Incest National Network) 24/7 hotline 1-800-656-4673

If you are feeling unsafe or experiencing thoughts of self-harm, please contact emergency services immediately in your area. Seeking support is not a sign of weakness. It is an act of protection and care.

References

The references that follow reflect the research, theory, and clinical scholarship that informed the development of this work. While this book is written in a narrative and applied style, it is grounded in established literature across counseling, psychology, trauma studies, and relational development. These sources are provided to support transparency, allow interested readers to explore the empirical and theoretical foundations more deeply, and acknowledge the scholars whose work has shaped the concepts discussed throughout this text.

Ahmed, M., Cerda, I., & Maloof, M. (2023). Breaking the vicious cycle: The interplay between loneliness, metabolic illness, and mental health. *Frontiers in Psychiatry*, *14*, 1134865. https://doi.org/10.3389/fpsyt.2023.1134865

Bowlby, J. & Tavistock Institute of Human Relations. (1982). Attachment and loss. In *Basic Books: Vol. I* (No. 83–71445; Second Edition). Basic Books. https://mindsplain.com/wp-content/uploads/2020/08/ATTACHMENT_AND_LOSS_VOLUME_I_ATTACHMENT.pdf

Bremner, J. D. (2006). Traumatic stress: Effects on the brain. *Dialogues in Clinical Neuroscience*, *8*(4), 445–461. https://doi.org/10.31887/dcns.2006.8.4/jbremner

Brown, W (2025). "Shattered innocence, scarred love: A phenomenological study on the effects of childhood sexual abuse of African American women on their romantic relationships." Order No. 31937022, University of Holy Cross, 2025. https://uhcno.idm.oclc.org/login?url=https://www.proquest.com/dissertations-theses/shattered-innocence-scarred-love-phenomenological/docview/3201918934/se-2.

Craig, A. G., Thompson, J. M. D., Slykerman, R., Wall, C., Murphy, R., Mitchell, E. A., & Waldie, K. E. (2018). The long-term effects of early paternal presence on children's behavior. *Journal of Child and Family*

Studies, 27(11), 3544–3553. https://doi.org/10.1007/s10826-018-1206-1

Depression (major depressive disorder) - Symptoms and causes. (n.d.). Mayo Clinic. https://www.mayoclinic.org/diseases-conditions/depression/symptoms-causes/syc-20356007

Doyle, C., & Cicchetti, D. (2017). From the cradle to the grave: The effect of adverse caregiving environments on attachment and relationships throughout the lifespan. *Clinical Psychology Science and Practice, 24*(2), 203–217. https://doi.org/10.1111/cpsp.12192

Finley, A. J., & Schaefer, S. M. (2022). Affective Neuroscience of Loneliness: Potential Mechanisms underlying the Association between Perceived Social Isolation, Health, and Well-Being. *Journal of Psychiatry and Brain Science, 7*(6). https://doi.org/10.20900/jpbs.20220011

Hawkley, L. C., & Cacioppo, J. T. (2010). Loneliness Matters: A theoretical and empirical review of consequences and mechanisms. *Annals of Behavioral Medicine, 40*(2), 218–227. https://doi.org/10.1007/s12160-010-9210-8

Kumari, V. (2020). Emotional abuse and neglect: time to focus on prevention and mental health consequences. *The British Journal of Psychiatry, 217*(5), 597–599. https://doi.org/10.1192/bjp.2020.154

McGee, R. E., & Thompson, N. J. (2015). Unemployment and depression among emerging adults in 12 states, Behavioral Risk Factor Surveillance System, 2010. *Preventing Chronic Disease, 12*, E38. https://doi.org/10.5888/pcd12.140451

McLanahan, S., Tach, L., & Schneider, D. (2013). The causal effects of father absence. *Annual Review of Sociology, 39*(1), 399–427. https://doi.org/10.1146/annurev-soc-071312-145704

Meston, C. M., Rellini, A. H., & Heiman, J. R. (2006). Women's history of sexual abuse, their sexuality, and sexual self-schemas. *Journal of Consulting and Clinical Psychology, 74*(2), 229–236. https://doi.org/10.1037/0022-006x.74.2.229

Powers, A., Ressler, K. J., & Bradley, R. G. (2008). The protective role of friendship on the effects of childhood abuse and depression. *Depression and Anxiety, 26*(1), 46–53. https://doi.org/10.1002/da.20534

Radell, M. L., Hamza, E. G. A., Daghustani, W. H., Perveen, A., & Moustafa, A. A. (2021). The impact of different types of abuse on depression. *Depression Research and Treatment, 2021*, 1–12. https://doi.org/10.1155/2021/6654503

About The Author

Dr. Whitney Brown, Ph.D., LPC, is a licensed professional counselor, professor, researcher, and author dedicated to advancing culturally responsive mental health care and trauma-informed practice. She is the founder of Avenue Counseling and Consulting, LLC, where she provides individual therapy and consultation focused on the realities and challenges experienced within marginalized communities.

Dr. Brown serves as a counselor educator at a Louisiana university, preparing emerging clinicians to understand trauma, diagnosis, and the complexities of human behavior with both rigor and compassion. Her academic and clinical work draws heavily from her research on childhood sexual abuse among African American women and its effect on romantic relationships, identity development, boundaries, and emotional functioning.

Dr. Brown earned her doctorate in Counselor Education and Supervision from the University of Holy Cross, New Orleans, LA. She also holds a master's degree in Clinical Mental Health Counseling and a bachelor's degree in Sociology, both from Southern University and A&M College, Baton Rouge, LA. As a clinician and educator, she integrates cultural context, narrative understanding, and evidence-based care into a unified approach that prioritizes healing as both emotional and generational work.

Outside of her work, Dr. Brown enjoys reading memoirs and psychology literature, spending time with family, traveling, gardening, and listening to music that inspires reflection. She is also passionate about mentoring young women. Her life and writing reflect the same belief that growth is an intentional process, whether nurturing a plant, guiding a client, or understanding one's own pain. Dr. Brown resides in Louisiana, where she continues her work as a therapist, educator, and advocate for emotional liberation and culturally grounded healing.

Website
https://www.avenuecounselingllc.com/

Stay in Touch With Me

Thank you for taking the time to read my story. Healing is never a solo journey. If you would like to stay connected, learn more about my work, or follow new writing and resources, you're invited to join the community.

Website
https://www.avenuecounselingllc.com/

Blog
The Healing Avenue (reflections on growth, identity, trauma, and emotional wellness)
https://www.avenuecounseling.blogspot.com/

Publishing & Book Updates
Eighth Avenue Publishing, LLC
Email: eighthavenuepublishing@gmail.com
Website: https://www.eighthavenuepublishing.com/
For updates on upcoming releases, events, and new book releases.

Professional & Speaking Inquiries
Email: avenuecounseling@gmail.com
For workshops, speaking, clinical training, supervision, and media requests.

Social Connection
Instagram: avenuecounseling
Facebook: Avenue Counseling and Consulting, LLC
LinkedIn: www.linkedin.com/in/avenuecounseling/

Also by the Author

The Emotional Backpack (COMING SOON)

Notes

www.ingramcontent.com/pod-product-compliance
Lightning Source LLC
LaVergne TN
LVHW041846070526
838199LV00045BA/1469